MILLER

To Bill Withuhn, in recognition of his vital role in the realization of the placing of one of Harry Miller's masterpieces in the care of the American people.

Laguna Seca
21 Aug 1993

On the end papers
There were three **Packard Cable Specials**: The old Leon Duray front-wheel-drive, number 21; the Ralph Hepburn car, number 18, and a rear-drive Miller 91 that was entrusted to Tony Gulotta. All were finished in violet and yellow, and were fitted with Duray-designed intercoolers, said to be the best next to Frank Lockhart's personal design.
GBC ex Leon Duray

MILLER

Griffith Borgeson

with the Smithsonian Institution

Motorbooks International
Publishers & Wholesalers ®

First published in 1993 by Motorbooks International Publishers & Wholesalers
PO Box 2, 729 Prospect Avenue, Osceola, WI 54020 USA

Design by Leydon Grafix

*Made possible in part by the Smithsonian Institution
by a grant from the Harold Rubin Fund*

Library of Congress Cataloging-in-Publication Data

Borgeson, Griffith.
  Miller / Griffith Borgeson
  p. cm.
  Includes bibliographical references (p.) and index.
  ISBN 0-87938-814-5
  1. Miller, Harry A. (Harry Arminius), 1875–1943. 2.
Automobiles. Racing—History. 3. Automobile engineers—United
States—Biography.
  I. Title
TL140.M548B67 1993
629.228' 092—dc20

Printed and bound in Hong Kong

Photograph credits
Abbreviations for photograph credits are as follows:

FMC—Ford Motor Company
FU—Frederick A. Usher
GB—Griffith Borgeson
GBC—Griffith Borgeson Collection
GRDC—Gulf Research and Development Company
IMS—Indianapolis Motor Speedway
LG—Leo Goossen

MD—Mark L. Dees
MR—Michael D. Rosen
RB—Riley Brett
SI—The Smithsonian Institution
SM—Strother MacMinn
TC—Taggart Collection
TW—Ted Wilson

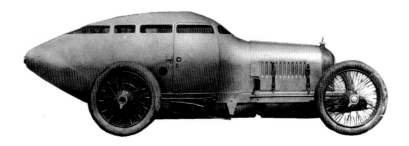

Contents

Harry Miller's **Golden Submarine** here in
bare aluminum in 1918, prior to painting.
MR/SM

To Robert M. Rubin,

a distinguished custodian of Harry Miller's patrimony

Packard Cable Special, 1992
The Smithsonian Institution Miller 91 ci front-wheel-drive race car. *Jeff Tinsley*

Bill
Now that you've
broken the ice,?
what's next?

Phil
@ MILLER
YEAR

Preface and Acknowledgements

I was born in Berkeley, California on December 21, 1918. A photo of which I am very fond shows me at the age of four and a half, gripping the steering wheel of my mother's Harry C. Stutz-built HCS phaeton. The winged emblem visible on its tire cover was identical to that on Tommy Milton's Miller 122, which won the Indy 500 that year, a fact in which I gradually learned to take pride. Berkeley was a fantastic town to grow up in, not only because of the local culture generated by the splendid university, but also because of that which emanated from the Hall-Scott factory, maker of fine aero and marine engines. Its guiding genius, Colonel Elbert "Al" J. Hall, remained forever faithful to the racing fraternity of which he had been a pioneer member in his youth. He had the biggest and best dynamometers on the west coast, and *The Berkeley Daily Gazette* kept its readers informed as to what celebrities of the racing world had come to consult with Al Hall. The great Fred Duesenberg and Harry Miller came to our town from time to time to discuss their problems with our distinguished citizen, their friend.

I came close to getting in on the ground floor of the automotive periodicals that began springing up in the early post-World War II years. I began writing for *Motor Trend* with its Volume 1, Number 1, of September 1949, soon moving to Los Angeles to join its editorial staff. Finding myself on Harry Miller's own turf, I set out to inform myself about this greatest of American racing-car builders. I was shocked to learn that, although he had died not even ten years before, the man and his achievements had been thoroughly forgotten not only by the public at large, but by the majority of the *passionnés* of the automobile in whose world I had the joy to live. So of course I went directly to the core of the problem, starting with Fred Offenhauser, Louis Meyer, and Leo Goossen, and what an incredible privilege that was.

I gradually came to meet many of Miller's other old associates, and even his widow and his son, and several of the drivers and mechanics who had shared his world. I learned much about that world, and about the sort of man that Miller had been. Everyone knew what his human failings were, but hardly anyone blamed him for them. By being himself, he enabled other men to rise above what they might otherwise have been, and to achieve things that were memorable. The memories that many of them cherished were a sort of wealth that they were privileged to possess and which gave

HCS-Miller 122, 1923
Tommy Milton at the wheel of the Harry C. Stutz Miller car with which he won the 1923 Indy 500. The cantilever rod under the frame rail was a Stutz or Milton touch to increase the rigidity of the frame.
GBC ex Tommy Milton

them a fulfillment which they bore with modest grace. Miller dreamed with open eyes and he enabled others to do the same. Which is precisely why I used verses by T. E. Lawrence and Ambrose Bierce at the opening of *The Golden Age of the American Racing Car* (Norton, Bonanza, 1966). Both verses deal with the dream-inspired hero, which was exactly the image that was communicated to me by most of those whose lives had been touched by the tranquil genius of Harry Miller.

I acknowledge their precious help, along with that of members of more recent generations who have been gripped to some extent by this tradition: Bradley, W. F.; Brett, Riley; Bromme, Lou; Bugatti, Roland; Burden, William A. M.; Burgess, John; Canestrini, Giovanni; Cord, Charles; Cord, Errett Lobban; De Alzaga, Martin; De Paolo, Pete; Duray, Leon; Elliott, Frank; Emmanuel, Victor; Freeman, Joseph; Goossen, Leo; Guyot, Andre; Hedrick, David; Hiroshima, Takeo; Houck, Jerry; Kiser, Karl; Kurtis, Frank; Laycock, Bob; Leto Di Priolo, Carlo; Leto Di Priolo, Dore; Ludvigsen, Karl; Marcenac, Jean; Merritt, Richard F.; Meyer, Louis; Miller, Edna; Miller, Eddie, Sr.; Miller, Ted; Milton, Tommy; Moskovics, Frederick E.; Offenhauser, Fred; Offutt, Eddie; O'Keefe, James; Olson, Ernie; Shaw, Wilbur; Smith, Clay; Sobraske, Walter; Sparks, Art; Sutherland, Robert De Lano; van Ranst, C. W.; Walton, Kenneth E.; Weisel, Zenas; Wallen, Dick; Walters, Bob; White, Bill; Winfield, Ed.

To say that special mention is due to Michael David Rosen is an extravagant understatement. I opened "The Pre-conquest Millers" in *Automobile Quarterly*, Volume 19, Number 1 (1981) with these words:

> In *The Golden Age of the American Racing Car* I told, in 1966, what I had been able to learn of the Miller/Offenhauser saga, which is without any parallel in automotive history. The years since then have brought to light a wealth of new knowledge which makes it possible to reconstruct the until-now hazy history of Miller before victory at Indianapolis in 1922 thrust international distinction upon man and marque. The foundation of this new grasp of how Miller attained that point is a herculean research operation which recently has been completed by Michael Rosen of San Francisco. Its object was the extraction, chiefly from the major newspapers of the Los Angeles and San Francisco Bay areas, but from myriad other sources, of all significant references, from 1904 onward, to the activities of certain key figures in automotive and aeronautical history. One of these figures of course was Harry Miller. Rosen also followed up innumerable promising leads, and one of them resulted in his discovery of a large collection of annotated photos, which had been preserved by one of Miller's close associates of the early days. With the technical assistance of a distinguished colleague, Strother MacMinn, Rosen was able to add photographic copies of this archive to his files. It bears mentioning that the automotive and aeronautical portions of what are best termed The Rosen Papers reflect only certain facets of this phenomenal researcher's interest in the history of mechanical transport.

The Rosen Papers have again been most valuable in the preparation of this volume. I am indeed privileged in having access to them.

This is but a brief introduction to the life and work of Harry Miller. The book, *The Miller Dynasty* (Barnes Publishing, Inc., 1981) by my friend of long standing, Mark L. Dees, is the monumental achievement in this field. First published in 1981, the entire press run was rapidly sold out. Now, more than ever, a new edition of this admirable work is mandatory. It has been most valuable in the preparation of this book.

A close friend and collaborator on Miller matters since the 1950s is Frederick A. Usher of Santa Barbara. He is particularly strong in the field of the iconography of our area of interest here, and has a vast collection of historic photographs, to which he brings analytical gifts which few possess. If he had done nothing more than restore to its pristine state and preserve for posterity the tattered remains of Leo Goossen's 9 ft long drawing of the TNT T4 engine, Usher's place as a historian of American automobile racing would be assured.

Brian Lovell, of Rye, England, is an engineer who has been involved with British racing engines since the early post-World War II years. He worked for Harry Weslake for years, after whose death he founded Weslake Developments Ltd. He is currently writing an analytical history of the racing engines of the last four decades. He is an old and dear friend, who has helped here with the table of technical characteristics for engines, above all with the calculations for brake mean effective pressure and mean gas velocity.

Credit is due to the Smithsonian staff in the Division of Transportation, National Museum of American History. William L. Withuhn is a Curator there, and for ten years, he has worked to develop the Smithsonian's small but *crème de la crème* collection of American racing cars. Gordon E. White has served as Auto Racing Advisor, and he played a key role in providing contacts to help implement NMAH's collection plan for competition vehicles, including the Hepburn *18*.

William Digney, of Fairfield, Connecticut, is a retired aircraft mechanic who has had a lifelong interest in open-wheel racing cars. He is a formidable researcher who has achieved an amazing knowledge of the histories of individual vintage American racing cars, which he has been wonderfully willing to share. For many years he has been a contributor to *The Bulb Horn* and *Cars & Parts*.

The family of Frederick Gibbs of New York City merits particular mention here, because of its role in the acquisition of the ex-Rubin Miller by the Smithsonian Institution.

I want to pay very special homage to Steve Earle for the vision and courage which he showed in selecting Miller as Marque of the Year in 1993 for his prestigious annual Vintage Car Races at Laguna Seca, Monterey, California. The marque, scarcely known to the world up to that time, has again become a living part of our culture. Thanks to Steve Earle. ■

Harry Miller, circa 1920
Miller's middle name, Arminius, was the Romanization of the name Hermann, the name of the German leader who so thrashed the invading Roman forces that they never tried again. Miller's first name well may have been Hermann, with Harry as a nickname. *GBC ex SM/RB*

Chapter One:
Harry Miller, the Custom-Built Man

Harry Miller, 1916
Miller pioneered the design of the twin-throat carbutetor. Jimmy Murphy's sojourn in Milan in 1923 may have provided Eduardo Weber with the principle that became famous with Weber carburetors.
MR/SM ex TC

Harry Miller was, quite simply, the greatest creative figure in the history of the American racing car.

His engines dominated American oval-track racing for almost half a century. Most of the speed records which there were to be had on land and water were held at one time or another by those engines. He created the school of American thoroughbred engine design which was faithfully followed by those who sought to outdo him. He was the originator, in the United States, of the racing car as an art object. He had a passion for metalwork and machinery that soared above and beyond all practical consideration. Parts of his machines that never would be seen by eyes other than those of the builders were formed and finished with loving care. His dedication to artistic and noble workmanship drew to his organization other technicians who believed in these same values. A whole sub-culture spread from the Miller nucleus, to become a permanent and integral part of innovative, artistic Southern California culture as a whole. It spilled over into the aircraft industry and it shook the automotive industry worldwide.

Miller created the first really streamlined closed car in the United States, and one of the first in the world. That was in 1917, and he was already telling journalists about using air-foil sections for improving the traction of super-light cars. He created unsupercharged engines of fantastic efficiency. Then he became the master of supercharging, achieving far more fantastic results, making the world passenger-car industry look archaic. He gave the world front-wheel-drive as a practical reality. He created really tractable and practical four-wheel-drive racing cars in the early Thirties, decades before almost anyone could appreciate the value of the principle. He always lived in the future, up to the time of his death, in 1943.

The Roots of Harry Miller

Harry Miller was born in Menomine, Wisconsin, on December 9, 1875. His father, Jacob Müller, had come from the town of Aschaffenburg in southern Germany. Jacob

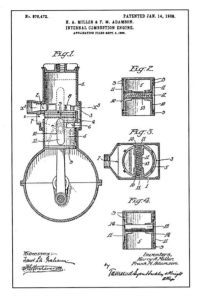

Miller Patent Drawing, 1908
Miller's mechanical creativity began early. Here is the drawing for a patent that he obtained in 1908. Miller shared the patent with Frank M. Adamson, an orphan whom he treated as his own son and who remained close to him until Miller left the west coast in the 1930s. *GBC*

Miller Test Car, circa 1917
This little Chevrolet runabout—probably thanks to Cliff Durant—was the test car of the "Miller Speed Emporium." Note the tall burette on the dashboard for measuring carburetor fuel consumption. *GBC ex MR/SM/TC*

had trained for the priesthood there, along with becoming a good linguist, musician and a superbly accomplished painter. In Menomine he married a Canadian girl named Martha Tuttle, and became a sort of intellectual farmer. Martha gave him three boys and two girls. During her pregnancy with Harry the American press carried stories about the completion of a huge monument in Germany, honoring a native chieftain, Arminius, who had put the Roman legions to rout once and for all, thus insuring the sovereign freedom of his own people. The name was the Romanization of the German name Hermann, which means chieftain. Jacob liked it and it became this son's middle name.

Harry did well enough in school in Menomine but as he told the story, when he was 13 he had had enough and wanted to become engaged in the real world. He loved everything mechanical and, dropping out of school, he went to work in a local brickyard, where there was a steam-driven donkey engine. A time came when the operator fell ill and Harry volunteered for the job. In spite of his youth he was given a chance, and he proved his ability both to operate and to maintain the big machine. He got the job, of which he was very proud.

According to the story, Harry worked at this job for a year, pretending to his family that he had been going to school. When his father, a stern man, learned the truth there was hell to pay, and the boy had to return to school. In 1892, when he was 17, he left home, and spent a year or so with his brother in Salt Lake City. There, and then for a year in San Francisco, he worked as a mechanic and machinist in bicycle shops. In 1894 he moved on to Los Angeles, where he met 16 year-old Edna Lewis, whom he married in 1897. He was 21 and making the good wages of $18 a week. He became fascinated by the new gasoline engines which were beginning to proliferate, and by the vehicles they propelled. In 1905, he was working for the Pasadena Automobile Company, living at 52 Delacey Street in that pleasant town, and built his own first car. It was primitive, with a dog clutch and single-speed transmission, but one can be sure that the workmanship was meticulous. His inventive gift began to manifest itself and early that year he filed for a patent on an original sort of spark plug. It was granted, and in 1906 he filed for two more, on ideas which he had developed with a certain Benjamin Gilbough. They were good enough to be bought outright by a man who soon became a director of the prestigious Peerless Motor Car Company. Miller met a much younger man, Frank M. Adamson, who shared his interests and values and with whom a most enduring friendship developed. That September, in association with two other inventors, they filed for a patent on an internal-combustion engine. It was granted in 1908 but seems not to have had a future.

In the meantime Miller had been developing an original design for an improved carburetor. He and his family lived in a house on Maple Avenue near Washington Street in Los Angeles. There was a long shed in the back yard which he named the Miller Carburetor & Mfg. Co. With the aid of a used lathe and drill press and a few essential tools, he began production. He filed for a patent to protect his carburetor design in January 1909 and received it that December, five days after his 34th birthday. His business career took off with a rush.

The Custom-Built Man

He stood about 5 ft 6 in, had blue eyes, black hair, fair complexion, ruddy cheeks, and red lips. For years in the Twenties and Thirties he wore the rather jazzy, sharply waxed mini-moustache which had been popularized by band leader Paul Whiteman. He was shy, silent, and reflective. He was in the habit of lying awake at night, while his brain worked. He did not waste much time on sleep. He had little to say, unless the topic should be machinery or, preferably, engines, in which case he could go on forever, with an interlocutor on his intellectual wave-length. Awesome authority that he obviously was, he was constantly being invited to address groups of one sort or another. His answer was always a polite and modest, "I'm sorry, but it's impossible."

Harry Miller was very tender and loving toward his wife, who was sweet and still very beautiful when I met her in 1953, when she was 62. He wanted to be a good husband to her and a good father to his son, but being so dedicated to and immersed in visions of the future and in burgeoning projects at work left precious little time for the cultivation of family relationships.

He had a fine mind and manifestly was a brilliant engineer. Bolting school, as he had done, had cost him dearly, and he was shy about that. As long as he was with his old team, he could always turn to a bosom friend when he got stumped by a problem. It was tough when he had to perform amidst knowledgeable strangers.

"He was a funny man," his wife said, meaning that he was clairvoyant. That frightened her and he, perceiving this, simply closed that door on her. He tried to discuss the subject with his son Ted, who was a teenager at the time. Ted didn't understand. "Someone's telling me what to do," he told intelligently sensitive Leo Goossen. "I have a control, and I count on it." When I asked pragmatic Fred Offenhauser if he thought that Harry, in leaving Los Angeles, had lost his 'control' he said, "Control, hell. He lost his team."

Money was unimportant to Miller as long as he had enough to eat and to finance projects. What his

Master Carburetor Ad, 1914
Miller created the Master carburetor, which became almost an essential part of a winning race car during the 'teens. *GBC ex MR*

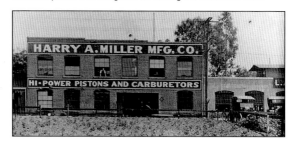

Miller Factory, 1915
Miller's Washington Boulevard plant was already a mecca for racing people from all over the United States, and the national clearing house for advanced technical ideas in the realm of high-performance machinery. *MR/SM ex TC*

Miller Factory, 1916
By this time Miller was a successful industrialist, designing and manufacturing carburetors, fuel pumps, aluminum-alloy pistons, and more. *TW*

3

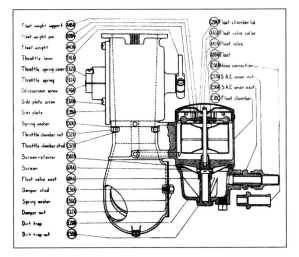

Miller Carburetor, 1917
Structural drawing of the Miller carburetor. *GBC ex MR/SM*

Miller Carburetor, 1922
Note the Miller "jet bar" or "fuel distributor." The jets were uncovered progressively as the barrel-type throttle valve opened. When it was wide open, there was zero obstruction in the venturi.
GBC ex MR

Miller Carburetor, 1928
The classic Type H of the 1920s. Note the jet bar and barrel valve.
GBC ex Floyd Clymer

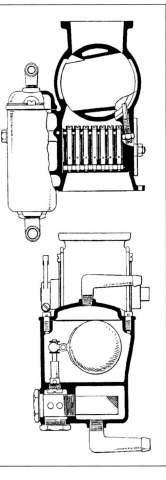

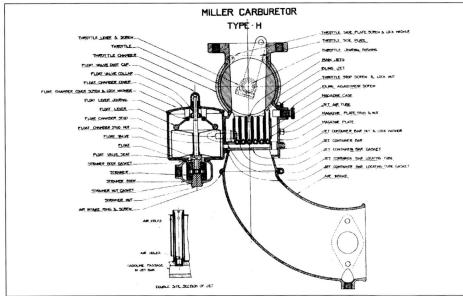

ultimate goal might have been, he seems never to have defined, for his family or for anyone else with whom I've spoken. He managed his money secretly. When Edna would ask him for some to put away in safety against a rainy day he would say something like, "Don't worry your head. I'll make some more." When it was suggested by friends that he put his ranch in the names of his wife and son, he shook his head stubbornly and said, "No. They might throw me out." In Edna's words, "He trusted no one."

He made several modest fortunes, all of which he spent liberally on friends and projects. He never gambled at gaming tables or on the stock market, but would always bet his last dollar on the drawing board on some imaginative new idea. He loved to entertain and he loved to have younger people around him. In the Twenties, when he had what he called his ranch—110 acres in Malibu Canyon, near Agoura, California—it was normal for him to receive fifty or sixty youthful members of the racing fraternity and their wives for a weekend. There was always food and drink in abundance.

The ranch also served for getting away from the crowd—for hunting (he was an excellent marksman), for meditating, for being alone with a key member of his team, such as chief designer Leo Goossen or plant superintendent Fred Offenhauser. He adored animals and kept a small zoo at the ranch. There were always two or three horses there. They were never ridden, but he enjoyed their presence and liked to talk to them. He always had a dog. It was his dog and it didn't stay at home, but went everywhere with him. He always kept the same parrot at liberty in the drafting room. It would talk, fly, attack visitors and otherwise generate atmosphere. And he never was without one or more monkeys. They would ride to work with him in his car and then animate the shop. In spite of his intense perfectionism, nothing delighted him more than to see a monkey messing up someone's work. It was a kind of boyish mischief in which he permitted himself to indulge to his very last days.

He was a wonderful boss, giving the members of his elite organization the feeling that they worked with Harry Miller, not for him. When someone would make a mistake in carrying out his directives he would blame himself for not having been adequately clear. He was noted for being almost infinitely patient with his collaborators, although there were unwritten rules of the house that should not be transgressed. One was that making a part so light that it would break was not to be criticized, whereas making anything that was unjustifiably heavy was beyond the pale. In the same spirit, no matter what part was designed, its form must be well-proportioned and harmonious, and its finish must always be fine.

Miller seemed to be indifferent to failure. Typically, when one of his men told him that he had just blown up a $5,000 engine on the test bench, Harry asked unperturbedly, "How bad?" "Total," was the reply. "Well," Miller said without batting an eye, "let's see how fast we can make a new one," and walked away. But that was nothing in comparison with his bankruptcy and loss of everything in 1933. When that happened, those closest to him could detect no emotional reaction whatsoever.

One could go on and on in describing this exceptional personality. His greatest character flaw, and one that everyone recognized, seems to have been that he remained interested in a given project until he conceived a new one. Then he would say to someone, "This is what I have in mind. You finish it." That could happen while the abandoned project was still on the drawing board. One of his associates, who loved him well, said, "He was a custom-built man, not a production man." ∎

Frank Adamson and Harry Miller, circa 1917
Adamson, left, became Miller's protégé in the early years of the century. He was a gifted technician, and held patents jointly with Miller. Through the years, he was a pillar of the company—and also of Offenhauser's revival. *GBC ex MR/SM/TC*

Peugeot GP, 1915
Dario Resta, left, discusses with Doc Caddy
the Miller carburetor on his 1914 Peugeot.
Few photos of this engine are known to
exist. *FU*

Chapter Two: The Era of the Burman-Peugeot

Peugeot GP, 1915
A 1914 Peugeot alongside the Pacific Electric Rail Road tracks in Santa Monica, California, during that year's running of the famous road race. *Archives Peugeot*

PERHAPS THE FIRST MENTION of a Miller carburetor is that which appeared in the *Los Angeles Times* for January 23, 1910. It was in the coverage of a pioneer air show which had just taken place in the small city. A highlight of the event was the excellent performance of the airplane of Glenn Curtiss, the engine of which had been equipped with a Miller car-type carburetor, but "built of aluminum" rather than of the customary heavy bronze. Then the May 11, 1910 issue of *The Horseless Age* announced that the Miller carburetor had just gone on the market and described its unusual concentric design. It soon began proving its virtues by being consistently on the winning cars in west coast races and on the engines of the most successful airplanes—those of Glenn L. Martin in particular. Miller's company and its assets were purchased by the sons of Teddy Roosevelt's vice president, Charles W. Fairbanks, and moved to their home town, Indianapolis, in April 1912. This company was incorporated as the New-Miller Manufacturing Company and the plant was claimed to have a production capacity of 70,000 carburetors per year. Miller could afford to buy his first production car, a Lozier. He, Edna, and Ted all suffered from the climate and they drove back to Los Angeles that November. Fairbanks' sons also bought the old Miller company in Los Angeles.

Miller continued to invent and file patents and in April 1913, he incorporated the Master Carburetor Company, for the manufacture and sale of a new and very different carburetor. The previously designed concentric gas reservoir gave way to one located conventionally at the side; the butterfly throttle valve was replaced by one of the barrel type, leaving the throat entirely unobstructed in full-open position. With brush-fire rapidity the Master came overwhelmingly to dominate racing in the West, and then spread all the way to the Atlantic Coast. It was a resounding commercial success in the passenger-car, aeronautical, and marine fields. It did so well that in April 1914, an Eastern financial syndicate purchased its national manufacturing and marketing rights east of the Rockies. The syndicate established the Master Carburetor

Miller Factory, 1920
The drafting room on Washington Boulevard, referred to as the Engineering Department. A young Leo Goossen is at the back of the room, wearing a white shirt. *GBC ex LG*

Leo Goossen, 1959
One of the stalwarts behind Miller, Goossen served as the chief designer for decades. By the 1950s, he had moved to the pattern loft of Meyer & Drake, where he was drawing Lance Reventlow's Scarab engine. *GB*

Company of America and by August had a large manufacturing plant in operation in Detroit. Miller retained his Western sales organization and returned to creative pursuits.

Not that he had been idle. Early in 1912, part-time metallurgist Miller had developed—with carburetor bodies in mind—an original blend of aluminum, nickel, and copper, which he called Alloyanum.

Continuing his experiments, Miller found that his new alloy was good for much more than light, strong carburetor bodies. He found that it made marvelous pistons and by about October 1913 he began pioneering their sale. All this was documented in the contemporary press. His pistons swiftly became a virtual necessity for high-performance and aero engines. And, in spite of the Master sale, he continued to design and fabricate special carburetors and inlet manifolds for high power output. These factors, plus a fine machine shop that could duplicate the most exotic parts, served to make the roomy plant of the Harry A. Miller Manufacturing Co. at 219 East Washington Street, between Maple Avenue and Los Angeles Streets, the west coast mecca for anyone and everyone in the country with an interest in optimum performance on land, water, or in the air. By 1915, at age 40, "Father" Miller had it made.

Alloyanum Characteristics			
Metal	Tensile Strength (psi)	Scleroscope Hardness	Specific Gravity
Alloyanum	49,600	24	3,532
Cast iron	20,000	28	7,248
Steel	55,000	30	7,854

The Miller-Christofferson Aero Engine

Back in the early fifties, Fred Offenhauser told me that "the first original Miller engine" was an in-line six which had been commissioned by San Francisco Bay Area aviation pioneer Silas Christofferson. Old racing driver Tommy Milton scoffed at this and insisted categorically that it was another famous pioneer, Lincoln Beachy, who had placed the historic order. Unable to obtain verification when writing *The Golden Age of the American Racing Car*, I accepted the persuasive Milton's story, only to learn from The Rosen Papers much later that Fred Offenhauser had been correct.

The order was a landmark in Offenhauser's career. He was a young toolmaker when hired by Miller toward the end of 1913. When Miller took on the Christofferson project early the following year he assigned a small spare room to it, baptizing it his Engine Department, and he put Offenhauser in charge of it. The engine had a single overhead camshaft, driven by shaft and bevel gears at the front, in the current aero Mercedes manner. The original concept called for building up the copper water jacketing of the steel cylinders by means of electroplating over wax. This proved to be perfectly feasible, but it was impractical in various ways. Miller finished by creating very elegantly sculptured cast-aluminum water jackets for this power plant. He innovated with fully enclosed valve gear, with pressure lubrication to the camshaft bearings and rocker arms, which was all very advanced. So was the special carburetor, which had one float chamber feeding two throats with each throat feeding three cylinders. Enhanced crankcase breathing and an oil radiator incorporated into the wet sump were also advanced features of this design. With bore and stroke of 4.75 by 6 in and a displacement of 638 ci the engine developed 120 bhp at 1400 rpm. In his *Aircraft Engine Encyclopedia* (1921) Glenn Angle reported, "A twelve-cylinder, which was a twofold likeness of the six-cylinder engine, is reported to have been developed." The Miller-Christofferson engine, which officially bore only the sponsor's name, was to have been manufactured in small series following the completion of the prototype in about April 1916. Then the sponsor was killed in a crash, and the project died with him.

The Burman-Peugeot

The next client of the Engine Department was dashing "Wild Bob" Burman, one of the very top drivers on the national level. One of the big problems with the Burman/Miller legend is that it was played back to me and others through Fred

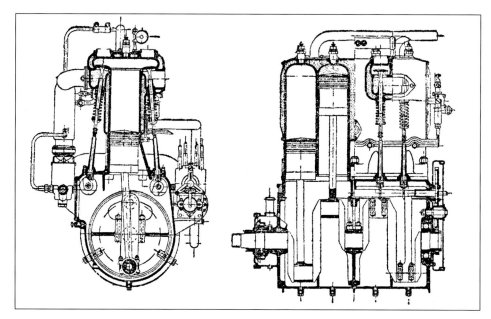

Labor-Aviation Engine, 1910
Conceived by the Swiss engineer Lucien Picker and drawn by Ernest Henry, the engine bristled with features that characterized Peugeot engines to come—and subsequently Miller engines. The Labor was a T-head, with its two camshafts in the crankcase and an external gear housing. *GBC ex Musée de l'Air*

Offenhauser's memory as a one-time happening that concerned the rebuilding of one single engine. We are saved again by the contemporary press. Having bought the 1913 Grand Prix Peugeot with which Jules Goux had finished fourth at Indianapolis in 1914, Burman enjoyed a great deal of success with this car. In fact, the papers were hailing him as "the world's fastest driver" when, on January 9, 1915, he was doing well in the Point Loma Road Race, near San Diego, when a connecting rod broke and tore up the Peugeot's lovely pioneer twin-cam engine. It took until February 2 for Burman to learn that any help from the Peugeot Import Company in New York, or from the war-harried factory in France, was out of the question. He turned to the Miller Speed Emporium, as the press liked to call it, where Dario Resta and his 1914 Peugeot were already in residence being

Miller Factory, 1919
The Miller plant at 17th and Los Angeles Streets. Parked in front is the small Chevrolet runabout that served as a piece of laboratory equipment for carburetion studies. *MR/SM ex TC*

9

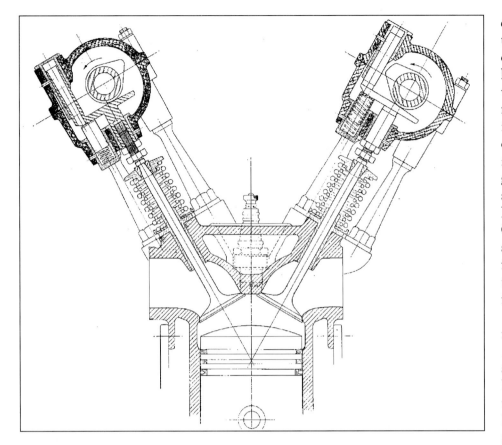

Peugeot GP Engine, 1913
What Miller found in the 1913 Peugeot engine marked him for life, as it also did Fred Offenhauser. There seem to be no Peugeot drawings in existence; this drawing was made by James Toensing based on the ex-Briggs Cunningham, current Collier Museum car.

did not miss this opportunity to increase the size of the already large ports. What they did to the general layout of the valve gear and its drive we do not know, other than that new and allegedly larger valves of tungsten steel were used. Offenhauser told me that the new engine "was not particularly similar to Peugeot practice." The photo of this new engine which appears in *Motor Age* for May 13 and 27, 1915, suggest a major departure from the Peugeot pattern. It shows, in fact, a structure that looks as though it had been made to receive a single overhead camshaft. Neither Fred Offenhauser nor Leo Goossen could give me any explanation for this striking anomaly. Further insight is obscured by the fact that no drawings are known to exist of either the Burman or Peugeot engines, so that we are forced to guess at their internal structure.

Parenthetically, there is on page 268 of Laurence Pomeroy's classic work, *The Grand Prix Car 1906–1939* (1949) a transverse section which is stated to be that of the 1913 GP Peugeot. It has been reproduced elsewhere many times as such. In reality, it has nothing to do with any twin-cam Peugeot, as comparison with photos will show at a glance. Its externally pivoted cam followers and narrow valve included angle seem to make it an early Frontenac.

To return to the Burman-Peugeot rebuild/re-design, the cylinder block casting was sufficiently complicated that the best foundries in southern California were unable to cope with it. It was most likely Miller's client E. J. Hall, of the Hall-Scott Motor Car Company in Berkeley, who made him aware of the remarkable qualifications of the Macaulay Foundry in the San Francisco area. From that time onward and in spite of the distance involved, Miller block castings were made at Macaulay's, as were the blocks for the Miller engine for the Leach passenger car and for practically all of the Offenhauser engines down through the ages. In the case of the Burman rebuild, the newspapers stated that two spare blocks were cast, in addition to the one which was put into immediate service.

While the rebuild was taking place Dario Resta won both the Vanderbilt Cup Race and the

tuned for the big races to be held in a few weeks in conjunction with the San Francisco World's Fair. The preparation of Resta's car included the installation of a Miller carburetor, inlet manifold, and a set of Alloyanum pistons.

Burman persuaded Miller to take on the job of building him an entire new engine, aside from the very few bits which could be recuperated from the scattered Peugeot. The two men, plus Offenhauser and draftsman John Edwards, pooled ideas for changes that it would be wise to make to the original design. To begin with, the displacement limit for the 1915 Indianapolis 500 was being reduced from 450 to 300 ci. So it was not merely a replacement cylinder block that was wanted, but one with very different dimensions of bore and stroke. The re-designers settled upon 3.625 x 7.10 in, a very long stroke-to-bore ratio of almost 2:1, and a displacement of 296 ci. The Peugeot's cylinder head was an integral part of its cast-iron block. The team

Grand Prix (the papers spurned efforts by the organizers to impose the Americanized name "Grand Prize") at San Francisco—700 bitterly fought miles against many of the best machines in the world. Resta's 1914 Peugeot was described as being "a wreck" when brought to Miller's to receive the total treatment. Piston and rod failures were problems that dogged the Peugeots and Arthur G. Hill, head of the Peugeot Import Company in New York, announced before leaving the Coast that the three Peugeots for Indianapolis would be fitted with Miller Alloyanum pistons.

For his new engine Burman, like Resta, took advantage of another Miller high-performance accessory: light but super-strong tubular connecting rods. They were of Miller's own design and he was already known for them in the racing milieu. They were made of chrome-vanadium steel, another alloy with which Miller was a pioneer. He and his team also made fundamental and much needed improvements in the somewhat folkloric Peugeot lubrication system. Although Miller was already working with multiple carburetor installations, he used a single Master in this case, along with an inlet manifold of his own design. New steering arms and knuckles (including wheel spindles) and front and rear axles were made and the Peugeot light-alloy rear-axle center section was replaced with one machined from chrome-vanadium billet stock. When the job was finished one journalist joked that only the frame and steering wheel of the original car remained unchanged.

The transformed machine had its first outing at speed at Los Angeles' famous Ascot Park on April 4, 1915, and it won the main event. Next, Burman entered and won an important 200-mile road race at Oklahoma City. He drove with a serenity that was quite alien to his traditional "Wild Bob" image and which apparently reflected the ease which he felt at the controls of a car which the papers said weighed 200 lb less and developed ten percent more horsepower than it had before its metamorphosis. Its next trial would be the 1915 Indy 500.

The car's satisfied owner tried to enter it as a

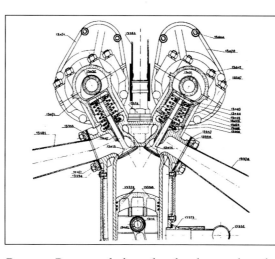

Ballot Engine, 1919
It is believed that the cup-type cam followers were first used by Ernest Henry, for the 1919 straight-eight Ballot. When Ralph De Palma asked Fred Offenhauser to work on his similar 3.0 liter Ballot in Los Angeles in 1920, Fred saw the cups and took the idea back to his employer, Harry Miller. *GBC ex Fernan Vadier*

Burman-Peugeot, feeling that he deserved credit for the changes he had wrought in it. The AAA-Contest Board, waging a battle against untruth in publicity, refused, listing the car simply as a Peugeot. Knowing that the car had been altered from stem to stern, Peugeot Import appealed this decision. It wanted Burman's name added to the car's title, not wishing to be held responsible for modifications made to the product by others. But the Contest Board refused to budge, decreeing on May 28 that "the general scheme of design underlying the various units of the car remain today to all intents and purposes as they existed when the car was originally sold by the said Peugeot company to the said Burman."

Wild Bob again took it easy, finishing in sixth place at the Speedway. During the balance of the season his only wins were in a 100-miler at Burlington, Iowa in July and in a 25-mile scuffle at Providence, Rhode Island in September. But on the same day at Providence he finished second in a 100-miler, and elsewhere during the season he racked up seconds in 100-milers at Kalamazoo and Sheepshead Bay, third for the same distance at Chicago, and fourth in a 350-miler at Tacoma. In other words, Bob Burman and his Miller-modified Peugeot were one of the country's most consistent top-money combinations. And then *The Los Angeles Examiner* for December 25 reported that Burman had "telegraphed Harry Miller to immediately start work duplicating his Peugeot motor...." He want-

GP Detail, 1916
The design of the original cam followers of the GP Peugeots was complex, costly to make, and difficult to work on. A French inventor, Albert Morin, conceived this consummately direct and simple cup-type cam follower. *Institut National de la Propriété Industrielle, Paris*

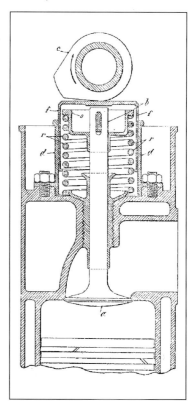

ed the new one to be ready for the George Washington Sweepstakes at Ascot on March 9, 1916.

The Miller-Oldfield Delage

While all this had been going on, Barney Oldfield had been experiencing nothing but frustration in his efforts to get a proper ride. Money was no problem and he had tried to get one of the new GP Mercedes out of Stuttgart on the eve of the war, but had the turf cut from under his feet by Ralph De Palma, who had gotten there first. By that time, all of the Peugeots had been snapped up and the only reasonably good prospect left was the 1914

desmodromic, twin-cam Delage. Barney received one of these cars from France in July 1915, and drove it to no avail at Chicago in August. And then, in the Astor Cup race at Sheepshead Bay at the end of September, he threw a rod and wrecked his engine. It says something about Miller's status at that time that "The Master Driver of the World" shipped his mount from New York to Los Angeles to receive Miller's intervention. This consisted of patching up the engine, fitting it with proper rods, light-alloy pistons, dual carburetors and manifolds, changing the front axle, and other unspecified modifications. In order to tune this engine proper-

Peugeot GP, 1913
Jules Goux won the 1913 Indy 500 impressively with his 1912 Peugeot. *IMS*

JULES GOUX - 1913 WINNER.

ly Miller had to familiarize himself intimately with the design and functioning of the Delage's unique desmo valve gear. The rebuild began in the latter part of October 1915.

It was still progressing slowly when Burman himself appeared at the Miller plant on January 10, 1916, to supervise the rapid progress of his latest project. On February 14, the *Los Angeles Times* noted his great good luck on two counts. The first was his having been signed by the Indianapolis Speedway to head its team of Premier-built replicas of the 1914 GP Peugeot. The second was that a group of Flint, Michigan businessmen had offered to finance a new car for Burman. This Flint Special, Bob told the press, would be a terrific car and he would campaign it in 1917. Burman had the need and the capital for a new engine of advanced design. Such a project may have been inaugurated at Miller's more or less simultaneously with the second rebuild of the Burman-Peugeot.

"The Motor Bob Never Saw Finished"

Miller had the ex-Goux car back in service in time for Burman to finish second in the important March 100-miler at Ascot. Then came his fatal crash at Corona. The papers called it "the most terrible accident in the history of auto racing in the West." The blow to Miller must have been great in a number of ways. For one thing, the *Examiner*

reported that Burman "was at work building in Los Angeles [read 'at Miller's'] a new car which he was to have driven at Indianapolis next month." It was Miller's popular field representative, C. J. Cadwell. better known as Doc Caddy, who accompanied Bob's body and widow back to Michigan, like a member of the family.

On May 19, Mrs. Burman was back in southern California to arrange for, among other things, the disposition of Bob's machinery. Ace motorsport writer Al Waddell explained in the *Times* for June 1 that this consisted of three different cars. One was the ex-Goux Peugeot, which had just been reconditioned by Miller for the third time. "The motors of the other two cars," Waddell said, "are built by Harry A. Miller of this city." The reader was left to wonder about the origin of the chassis in which they were installed.

In the Rosen/MacMinn photo trove there is an excellent view of a twin-cam engine, the water-jacket plate of which bears the Burman name. It is in much smaller letters than those which were used for the original rebuild, as shown in *Motor Age*. It is a very different engine from that one and from any other twin-cam engine of the time. This is because it anticipated the total enclosure of valve gear which would be introduced by Ballot in 1919.

Written below the photo are the words, "The motor that Bob never saw finished." ■

Miller-Burman Engine, circa 1916
"The motor that Bob never saw finished." Its enclosed valve gear alone made it an important improvement over the GP Peugeot that inspired it. *MR/SM ex TC*

Barney Oldfield, 1917
The cigar-chewing Oldfield was one of the
great legends of American auto racing. He
commissioned construction of the Sub
near the end of his career as a driver. *MR/SM
ex TC*

Chapter Three: Miller, Oldfield, and the Single-Cam Fours

Barney Oldfield and the Golden Submarine, 1918
With his cigar firmly clenched in his jaw, Oldfield climbs inside the Sub at the Ascot racetrack, Los Angeles. *FU*

O N JULY 30, 1916, the *Los Angeles Times* told of a new, all-Miller engine which had been under development in the greatest secrecy "for the last seven months," which would put its inception at about the time of Burman's Christmas telegram. It was stated that this new Miller engine was being built for long-time De Palma mechanic Tom Alley, now a driver in the big time himself. Technical details were limited to say that it would be a 16-valve four, good for about 150 bhp at 3000 rpm. It was being "constructed of Miller metal extensively," no doubt meaning of Alloyanum. This description fits the Miller "all-aluminum" design which made its appearance in 1917. It could have been used equally well to describe the apparent bridge between Miller's past design practice and that which was to come. That bridge was his little-known Iron Four.

This seemingly one-off engine was pictured in the *Times* of November 12, 1916, wherein it was said to have been completed sixty days previously, when it was shipped to Chicago upon receipt of a $4000 check. The purchaser may have been the new Pan-American Motor Company, Tom Alley's sponsor. The Rosen/MacMinn photos include sharp views of the front, rear, and both sides of this engine, which is immediately identifiable by its black cylinder block. The light-alloy waterjacket plate on the inlet side bears the Miller name in rather old-fashioned, curving script, such as Duesenberg was using at that period. The barrel crankcase is of the Peugeot type, and a train of narrow spur gears runs up the front of the block to drive a single overhead camshaft. There is a magneto on either side of the dual ignition engine and there is a separate port for each of the eight inlet valves, unlike the low-velocity gallery-type ports of Peugeot practice. One naturally wonders if this project may not have been based upon the adaptation to sohc of one of the Burman spare blocks, but the visual evidence discourages this view. Again the valve gear is totally enclosed, and what is most striking about the engine is its clean elegance, a Miller hallmark. The *Times* credited it with 135 bhp.

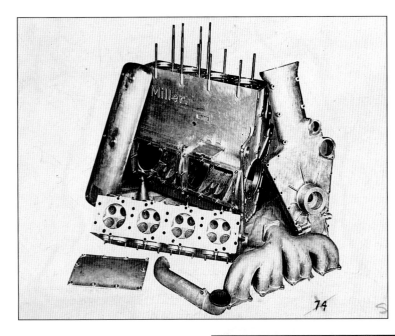

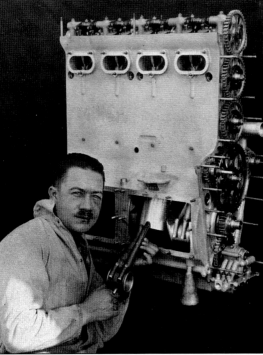

Miller Four Sohc, 1916
Prominent racing driver of the day, Roscoe Sarles, removes a piston and rod assembly from the bottom end. For great ease of maintenance, the rods and pistons could be installed or removed through huge hand-holes. In a period when exposed valve gear was almost universal in overhead-valve engines, this was one of the cleanest designs in the world. *GBC ex TW*

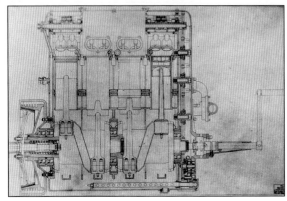

The Golden Submarine

On September 3, 1916 the papers blared that the great Oldfield had given up on his Delage engine and that he had ordered a new one from Harry Miller with which to replace it. In the blaze of The Master Driver's fame, Tom Alley and his plans simply vanished from the automotive news. Oldfield hoped to have the new combination ready in time for the Vanderbilt Cup and Grand Prix races which were to be held in Santa Monica on November 16 and 18. But that target was not met and suddenly it was February 2, 1917, and a *Times* headline read, "Three Miles a Minute in Gassified Submarine." It said that Oldfield was having two new cars built by Miller, one a more or less conventional *bolide* for

(*above*)
Miller Four Sohc, 1916
End view with the Miller updraft barrel-valve carburetors at left.

(*above left*)
Miller Four Sohc, 1916
Side view of the four-cylinder with the dual exhaust ports.

(*left*)
Harry Miller, 1917
Miller, here with one of his all-aluminum sohc four-cylinder engines, at a youthful 41 or 42. Note the clean, sculptured form of this creation. *MR/SM ex TC*

The Golden Submarine, 1917
The Sub, with its mirror-like gold lacquer finish, brand new and sparkling. *GBC ex TW*

road and track racing. The other would have a mysterious "submarine" (it was wartime, and u-boats were big in the mass mentality) body and would be capable of something like 180 mph. The world Land Speed Record stood at 124.

A few more details were released two days later. First of all, the conventional car would be the much-modified Delage chassis, fitted with a streamlined, closed body. That was an absolute first in world history, unless one cared to count the marvelous but forgotten Baker electric streamliner of 1902. Some races still were being held for the old 450 ci class, and the car would accept such an engine as well as its normal one of 300 ci. Or, to be more precise, of 289 ci, the result of its Burman-like 3.625 x 7.00 in bore and stroke.

"For special straightaway work," an article read, "Barney is going to install in another car of the same type a twelve-cylinder aeroplane motor being made by Harry Miller for De Lloyd Thompson, the aviator, for a special plane being built at the shops of the Standard Aeroplane Company of New York. This great motor will develop 300 hp at 1600 rpm with 5 in bore and 6 in stroke, and yet weighs only 600 lb." The entire car would weigh about 1600 lb.

In the meanwhile, Tom Alley had made it back into newsprint. On January 11 the *Examiner* noted that he was building a racing car for Pan-American, that it would use the new Miller Old-

field-type aluminum engine, which could be converted from 300 to 450 ci and vice versa with about two hours' work.

More details on the spectacular Oldfield projects appeared in *Motor Age* for February 22. One learned that the motives for adopting the closed body were related as much to safety in case of over-turning as they were to streamlining, and a roll bar or cage seems to have been part of the structure. Another safety-inspired feature was "double steering," with a separate drop arm and drag link for each front wheel.

Traction problems due to the light weight of the record machine were anticipated by its designers, Miller and Oldfield. Barney was quoted as saying, "If deflecting planes will drive the airplane up and down according to their angle, why won't a deflecting plane on a car going more than 100 mph help drive it down to the ground and add weight and aid in the traction?" The author of the article stated that he had seen the two new chassis under construction and that the engines were nearly finished. *Motor Age* printed photos, perhaps for the first time, of the one-piece block/crankcase castings of both the four and the twelve. Each was as refined in concept as it was original.

Week after week the newspapers carried superficial news of these projects but it took until April 26 for the first proper technical description of the four to appear, simultaneously in *The Automobile* and in *Motor Age*. Here at last one learned that the engine employed wet steel cylinder liners—the world's first, at least among racing engines. It had four valves per cylinder and they seated directly against the light alloy of the detachable cylinder head. The valves formed a 30 degree included angle and were actuated by a single overhead camshaft. It, in turn, was driven by a train of five ball-bearing-mounted spur gears. The two-piece crankshaft ran in three large ball races, the camshaft was hollow and carried oil under pressure to the valve gear, and the connecting rods were tubular. The article stated, "The cam unit deserves special attention in that there are extra follower cams which mechanically return the forked rocker arms, each of which oper-

ates two valves. This makes the rocker positive in its return, independent of the spring action." Miller obviously had been impressed by the desmodromic valve gear of the 1914 Delage, but his way of achieving the same effect was original, using mechanically actuated rockers instead of stirrup cam followers, along with a very light valve spring for final seating of the valve. He did not bother to patent any part of this engine.

Its 360-degree main-bearing supports were integral parts of the cylinder block. There were no external oil or water pipes, all such plumbing being part of the block casting. Magnetos on each side of the block, driven by the first idler cog in the gear tower, provided the voltage for two spark plugs per cylinder. The engine had just been found to give 135 bhp at 2950 rpm on a Sprague water-brake dynamometer. This translated as 28.5 bhp per liter which, for a beginning, compares not at all badly with the 30.7 of the twin-cam Sunbeam six of 1916 and the 29.1 of the also twin-cam Ballot straight-eight of 1919. The exceptionally long stroke/bore ratio of 1.93 : 1 happened to be identical to that of the Sunbeam just mentioned, which probably also had passed through Miller's hands and under his scrutiny at least once. He had already developed a 2:1 reduction gearbox for turning aircraft propellers at reasonable speed. With a pound-to-bhp ratio of 3.3:1, the sohc Miller four was perfectly competitive with many

good aero engines of the period.

The *Times* for April 8 told that the Alley engine was coming along, and that local road-racing driver A. A. Cadwell (relationship with Doc Caddy undetermined, but presumed close) had ordered one for himself. He was a cameraman for D. W. Griffith and may have helped to finance the entire project, Sub and all. The first photo of the Sub, which was already nationally famous, appeared in the May 8 issue of the *Times*, and it merited every square inch of the near half page that was allotted to it. On the 20th, one learned that testing of the Alley engine was almost complete and that the Cadwell order for an engine had turned into one for a complete car. By June 3, the Sub had been painted "gold bronze" and on the 5th it was shipped to Oldfield in Chicago. It was chaperoned by Frank Elliott, a young mechanic and driver who enjoyed Miller's confidence.

The new car created a tremendous sensation but was plagued by constant teething troubles and dropped out of the June 16 250-miler on the Chicago Riverview board speedway very early. The Miller-engined Oldfield Delage was a different story, however. It went the whole distance and finished third, driven by Cliff Durant, the son of General Motors' founder William Crapo Durant and himself the greatest patron that motorsport in the

The Golden Submarine, 1917
Rear view of the Sub showing its bullet-shaped tail where the engine exhaust was discharged. *GBC ex TW*

Harry Miller and the Golden Submarine, 1917
Posed at the back entrance of Miller's Washington Boulevard plant. This was a light industrial part of town where, as one sees, there were motion picture-related businesses. Miller's client, A. A. Cadwell, who had worked with Thomas A. Edison on cinematographic projects before he became a cameraman for D. W. Griffith, may have been associated with one of shops. *MR/SM ex TC*

Miller Aero V-12, 1917
Drawing of the V-12 aero engine. The ingenious camshaft and valve layout anticipated Packard and Lycoming practice of the 1930s. *MR/SM ex TC*

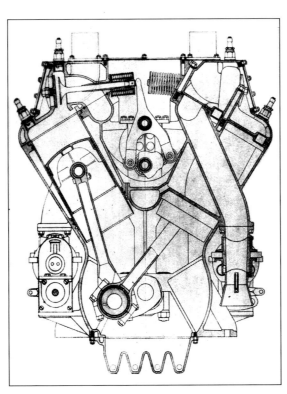

Miller Aero V-12, 1917
The engine was absolutely outstanding for its extreme cleanliness. *GBC ex TW*

United States has ever had. A week later, at Milwaukee, Oldfield had the Golden Submarine sorted out well enough to trim Ralph De Palma in 10, 15, and 25 mile match races and to break "all records for these events." Miller's career as a car builder began with the Sub, as Oldfield's career as a driver drew to a close with it. The car itself remained on the active list until 1920.

The A. A. Cadwell car was completed in time to finish in the money in a big race at Omaha on July 4, 1917. The 112.5-miler at Uniontown, Pennsylvania on September 18 was a red-letter day for Miller because the Sub, its topless Cadwell twin, and the Oldfield Delage all took part. And the latter car actually won, driven by Frank Elliott. On October 13, Tom Alley won a 20-mile sprint on the two-mile saucer at Chicago with the Miller-engine Pan-American. On November 29 a reported 30,000 spectators at Ascot witnessed Barney and the Sub set a new all-time record for the dirt-track mile. And on January 13, 1918, after Barney had had at least two close brushes with death in his closed car, he stripped it of its marvelous egg-shaped body for another go at Ascot. In this brutalized form the naked Sub won two of the three main events that day, and set a new absolute record for ten miles on dirt. Harry Miller had not done too badly. His first car was probably the fastest dirt-track machine in the world. It's a shame that the Sub configuration never had the opportunity to show its worth on the straightaway, using the big V-12 engine as planned.

Wartime Miller Aero Engines

The V-12 1414 ci mammoth reputedly had undergone a 100-hour test at the factory, after which it was shipped to McCook Field at Dayton, Ohio for testing by the Bureau of Aircraft Production. Rosen located a copy of the report of the tests, which took place between January 15 and 25, 1918. Repeated problems were encountered which resulted from leakage of cooling-system water past the rubber o-ring seals at the ends of the cylinder sleeves, and Miller decided to pursue the project no further. It had been conceived for small-volume

production before the United States had entered the war. Now Detroit was into that sector on an industrial scale, and various large European aero engines were being manufactured in volume, even in the United States. Both the present and early postwar markets had been shot down.

Manufacturing rights to the Miller aluminum four as an aero engine were obtained in 1917 by the Fitchburg (Massachusetts) Machine Works. In his *Airplane Engine Encyclopedia* (Dayton 1921) Glenn Angle listed a bore and stroke of 4.00 x 7.00 in. Rated horsepower—that approved for continuous operation—was given as 125 hp, with 139 hp obtainable at 2600 rpm and 155 hp at 2900 rpm. The latter figure would equal 29 bhp per liter and, with a reported dry weight of 410 lb, 2.64 lb per hp—figures which were not bad at all for the time. But the military need for such small engines was drying up. It is not known that Fitchburg ever manufactured a single Miller engine. One in mint condition was found there in 1969 and acquired by well-known collector and author Richard F. Merritt. It almost certainly is a Miller-built specimen on which the contract with Fitchburg was based. Married to parts from the reputed ex-Oldfield car engine, it became the heart of today's splendid Buck Boudeman-built replica of the Golden Submarine.

Miller also received a commission from local developers to build a smaller version of the sohc aluminum four to power what was called an aerial torpedo or flying bomb. It differed from the normal type in employing a shaft-and-bevel camshaft drive.

One of the European aero engines which was to be manufactured industrially in the USA was the

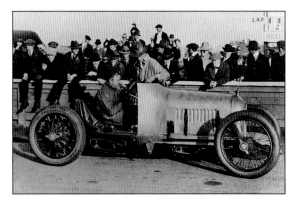

Cadwell Miller Four, 1917
Miller built a twin to the Golden Submarine in 1917, but fitted it with an open body. This twin was constructed for A. A. Cadwell. From left, ace mechanic Claude French, Miller, and Cadwell. *FU*

Cadwell Miller Four, 1919
Cadwell's car had the same system of double drag-link steering as the Sub. This photo records the first racing use of hydraulic brakes. These were of the external contracting type that were in general use at the time, although front-wheel brakes of any kind were extremely rare and highly controversial. *MR/SM ex TC*

infamous Bugatti U-16. Fred Offenhauser told me that "there was a party in New York named Brown who got this big Miller carburetor contract [for the U-16], which provided that the carburetors had to be made in the east, near the engines." Miller, presumably leaving his affairs in the competent hands of his protégé and partner, Frank Adamson, moved to New York City in May 1918. There he established the Miller Products Company, at 109 West 64th Street, near Broadway. In addition to carburetors, Miller-designed fuel pumps also were made, Offenhauser told me, for several manufacturers of aero engines. Following the Armistice, in November, and the cancellation of the U-16 and Liberty engine programs, it took Miller until the following February to wind up his affairs in the east and return to Los Angeles.

Legacy of the Golden Submarine

In Los Angeles, the *Examiner* for March 10, 1918 announced that driver Eddie Pullen was coming out of retirement to drive a machine owned by one Addison Brown. "The car is almost a duplicate of the Oldfield speed creation," the item read. "It is equipped with the aeroplane type motor. . . . The car was a sensation when driven in the east by Gil Anderson, Oldfield, too, handled it at Uniontown and made one of the fastest laps

ever recorded there. . . ." In the Rosen/MacMinn photos the Miller Iron Four is labelled "Pullen's engine." Also in that collection are photos of a car which is the Cadwell machine, painted white and fitted with hydraulic front brakes. The car ran in the last of the Santa Monica Road Races, in 1919, making, according to Ed Winfield, the first known appearance of such brakes on a racing car in competition. It had to drop out of the contest when its hydraulic fluid leaked away, causing Miller to suspend his pioneering experiments with Loughead/Lockheed. The photos are labelled simply "Miller Racing Car 1917" which, if correct, shows that Miller was into this field of experimentation at that early date.

On June 22, 1918, there was a 100-miler at Chicago in which Oldfield and the Sub were joined by none other than De Lloyd Thompson at the wheel of the Oldfield Delage. Also present was a West Coast driver, Omar Toft, in command of the first car to bear the name Miller Special. Mark Dees identifies it as the ex-Cadwell machine. Then the Miller name was out of the racing news until January 19, 1919, when the *Times* ran a photo of the same Toft car, ready for a romp at Ascot. The paper also noted that Eddie Pullen was to be Cliff Durant's relief driver in a Chevrolet Special in the coming Indianapolis 500. ∎

Cadwell Miller Four, 1919
The Cadwell car was repainted in late 1917 and featured the Miller airfoil emblem low on the cowl. This bit of symbolic ornamentation was used on other Miller cars—and even showed up on the one-off Auburn Cabin Speedster of 1929.
MR/SM ex TC

Miller Baby Chevrolet, 1920
The earliest photo of Cliff Durant's Baby
Chevrolet, taken at the Beverly Hills board
speedway in February 1920. *FU*

The Vital Early
Chapter Four: **Role of Cliff Durant**

Miller Baby Chevrolet, 1920
Front view of Cliff Durant's Baby Chevrolet.
The car was built for the 3.0 liter formula
that went into effect that year. *FU*

THE CHEVROLET MARQUE had been created by Cliff Durant's
father as a weapon for the reconquest of General Motors, from
which vast empire he had been ousted. Cliff had been placed
in charge of Chevrolet's fortunes in the western states. It was
there that the new marque's real success had begun, with
Cliff's brilliant performance with one of the little cars in the
Los Angeles-Phoenix Desert Road Race in 1914. The car
probably was Miller-equipped and tuned. Cliff was Los Ange-
les-based at the time and it just happened that Miller's test car
at that general period was a very snappy little cutdown Chevy
with a bolster fuel tank. It, too, is in the Rosen/MacMinn photos.

In 1915, Cliff purchased one of Stutz' last-year's works-team racers, modified it to
suit his own ideas, christened it a Chevrolet Special, and went about doing for the marque what Burman and his teammates had done for Buick a few years previously. By 1919
Cliff had risen to be general manager of all Chevrolet operations in the west, which
were tremendous, but he still continued to race, "for relaxation," he said. For the March
15 Santa Monica Road Race he bought the ex-Gil Anderson Stutz—the fastest American car at Indy in 1915—and it, too, became another "Chevrolet Special."

The race held at Ascot on January 26 had been won by a four-cylinder Duesenberg-engined Roamer driven by Roscoe Sarles, former mechanic to Eddie Rickenbacker. Toft and the Miller Special finished second. Toft then renamed his car the
Ascot Special and entered it for Santa Monica. Another entry for that historically
important contest was Frank Elliott's in an Elliott Special which the papers described
as "another Miller-motored machine." We do not know if it was old or new nor if its
chassis also was Miller-made. As for the outcome of the 250-mile road race, victory
went to Cliff Durant and his Chevrolet Special.

Other news that spring referred to the rebuilding of the Sub by Roscoe Sarles and
Waldo Stein and its entry as an Oldfield Special at Indianapolis, Sarles to drive. Toft
also was entered there. He had changed his car's name one more confusing time, and
persisted with the hydraulic brakes which he had used at Santa Monica. And the *Times*

Miller-Durant Special, 1923
Jimmy Murphy at the wheel of one of the eight Miller 122s owned and campaigned by Cliff Durant. Miller finished third at Indy in 1923 and won the AAA National Championship. *SI*

for May 4 mentioned for the first time a Leach Special and said that "a few of the new cars will very soon be ready for delivery." The new cars referred to were products of the Leach Biltwell Motor Company, recently organized by local coach-builder (he made the Sub body) and car dealer Martin Leach. The Leach Power Plus Six was to have a sohc engine designed by Harry Miller. The Leach Special may have been a tentative new name for the old Sub, which was being rebodied at the time in the Leach plant. It retired with a broken rocker arm when the Indianapolis race was only eight laps old, while Toft completed 44 laps before throwing a rod.

The Miller 183 Four

The 300 ci formula would end with 1919, giving way to a new breed of three-liter, 183 ci machines. The Los Angeles press missed the next item, but it was picked up in Oakland, home base since 1916 of Cliff and of Chevrolet in the West. There the *Enquirer* of August 9 let it be known that "a fleet of 183 ci racing cars" was being built for Cliff Durant, "who intends to get to France to compete in the French Grand Prix next spring . . . accompanied by Hearne and possibly Eddie Pullen. . . ." This probably meant that Cliff had ordered three new cars from Miller.

One of Rosen's super-finds was Miller's US Design Patent, number 55,070, filed on September 22, 1919. As the accompanying repro-

duction shows (*page 27*), it contained some startling ideas. The double steering and cantilever rear springs of the first generation Millers were there, along with four-wheel brakes and lightened brake drums. There were the Bugatti flat-spoke wheels, five years ahead of Bugatti. Aft of the firewall was the profile of what would become the classic shape of American oval-track race-car bodies for at least a couple of decades to come. Anchored to the firewall was a fantasy engine which served to illustrate the use of the engine as a stressed chassis member, to which the front axle and suspension were attached. In other words, modern Formula 1 practice, turned around. The engine appeared to utilize three downdraft carburetors about a decade ahead of their time. Its symmetrical twin exhaust systems suggest anticipation of the stagger-valve principle which would make certain DO Fronty setups the terror of the dirt tracks in a decade or so.

The TNT and T4 Engines

Back in the 1950s Leo Goossen had told me of the TNT car and its engine. Drawing the latter had been his first big job with Miller. Miller had the idea of building a sports car, the engine of which would eliminate the need for a hood. The car would be called the TNT and its engine the T4. The engine's displacement would fit the upcoming 183 ci formula. As Leo understood it, the project was financed by Eddie Maier, prominent sportsman and owner of the big Los Angeles brewing company of that name. He was almost certainly on good terms with Cliff Durant. Leo had the impression that one engine had been built but did not know if it ever had been thoroughly tested.

This engine was the bridge between the sohc and dohc Millers. The big difference between it and its forerunners was its adoption of the Peugeot-derived Ballot top end, with twin cams, cup-type cam followers, centrally located plugs and all the rest. It was the world's first twin-cam engine to use light-alloy construction

along with wet cylinder liners. Goossen told me that he thought that the project fell through when Maier withdrew his financial support. His reason for having done so could have been disappointment in the engine. Leo himself was critical of the length of its connecting rod, the thinness of its cylinder sleeves, and the appearance of its radical chain drive to the camshafts. Leo's presentation ink drawing is dated August 1920, when the Miller 183 four already was an outcast. The original working drawings must have been made during the previous year.

On January 11, 1920, *The Oakland Tribune* reported that Cliff had "just wired his entry for the coming May's 500 from Oakland where, in the Chevrolet factory, a special 183 ci flyer is being build. . . ." Sports writer Al Waddell had become Cliff's public relations director and press agent. His words probably meant that it had been ascertained that there would be no French Grand Prix in 1920, and that the Durant commitment for three new Millers had been reduced to a single car for Cliff to drive on home ground.

In spite of his playboy reputation Cliff worked hard at many enterprises in addition to running Chevrolet's western empire. At this period he was

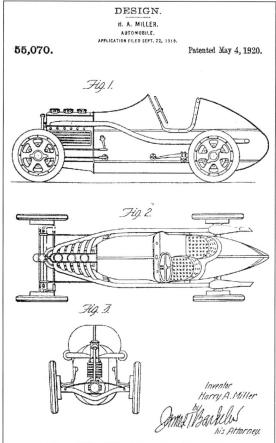

DESIGN.

H. A. MILLER.
AUTOMOBILE.
APPLICATION FILED SEPT. 22, 1919.

55,070.

Patented May 4, 1920.

Fig. 1.

Fig. 2.

Fig. 3.

Inventor
Harry A. Miller
by
James *Bartlow*
his Attorney.

Miller TNT, 1920
The Miller-built TNT, with cast-aluminum body. *ex David Hedrick*

Miller Design Patent Drawing, 1920
The famous Miller design patent, applied for in 1919 and granted in 1920. The body fixed the form of American track-racing cars for years to come. It also closely resembles the cast-aluminum TNT, which was to have no engine hood. Note the four-wheel brakes, double drag-link steering, and cantilever rear springs. The engine was strictly fantasy…probably. This forgotten document was discovered by researcher Michael Rosen. *MR*

27

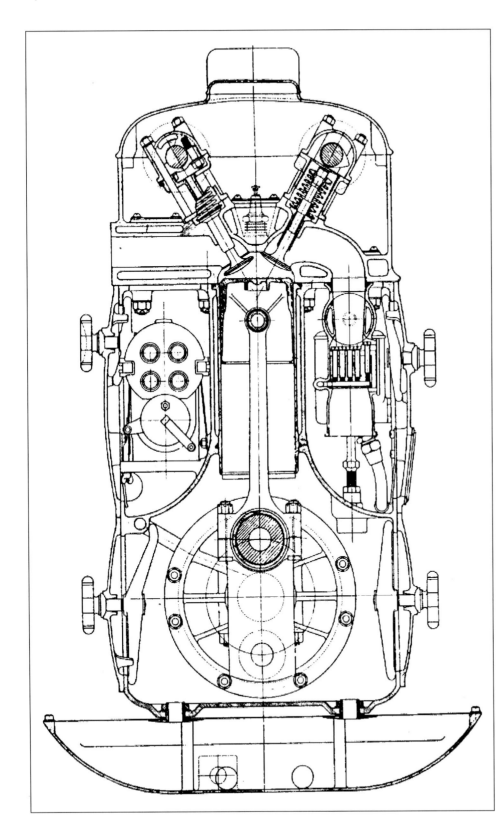

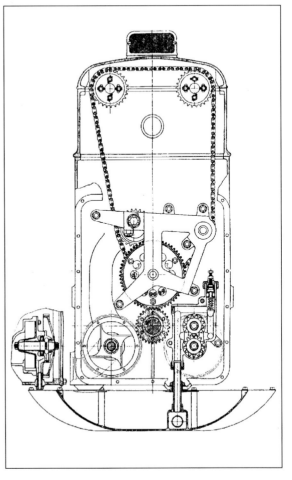

heavily into aviation, was establishing a pioneer western airline, and was occupied with the construction of airports, including Durant Field in Oakland. He was also profoundly involved in making the West Coast "the car racing capitol of the world" with, for a start, a chain of fine board speedways at Beverly Hills, Fresno, Cotati (near Santa Rosa), and Tacoma. The palatial Beverly Hills track opened on February 28 with a 250-miler. Cliff, in his new Miller-built 183 Chevrolet Special (it was called the Baby Chevrolet to distinguish it from the Stutz of the same name), was the first away at the drop of the starting flag, but his car ran disappointingly. Tommy Milton's former mechanic, Jimmy Murphy, won at the wheel of a Duesenberg single-cam straight-eight. Ira Vail, "the doughty ex-captain of the Hudson team," had acquired a

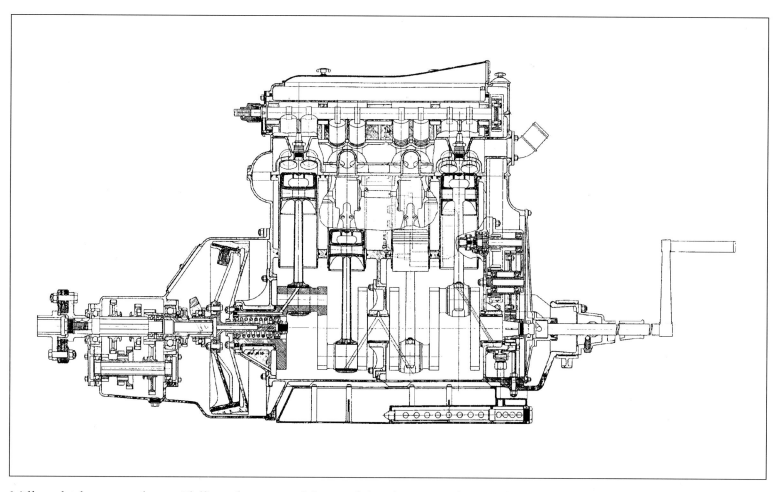

Miller which was similar to Cliff's and ran no better.

Four Millers were entered for the Memorial Day race at Indianapolis: the Sub, with its Leach-built speedster body; two cars called TNT, to be driven by Elliott and Alley; and the Baby Chevrolet, to be driven by Cliff. None of these cars seems to have arrived at the Speedway, the reason presumably being that, after their early entries, all were found to be non-competitive performers and were withdrawn. It has been assumed that all were powered by the same scaled-down version of the honorably performing 289 ci single-cam four. Not long ago Fred Usher, in studying photos of the Baby Chevrolet that were taken at Beverly Hills, noted the unmistakable crankcase sump which is pictured in Goossen's T4 drawings. Perhaps T4 sponsor

Maier withdrew his support because (1) the more advanced engine was passed to Durant without his approval or (2) it proved to be as uncompetitive as the single-stick 183.

To add to this enigma, there are two additional elements. First, on page 57 of his book, Mark Dees says "We're reasonably certain that this is the engine of the Miller-built Baby Chevrolet. . . ." Rather, it is the Iron Four of *The Los Angeles Times* of November 12, 1916.

Second, I have a letter from Fred Offenhauser in which he states, "We never built a single-cam 183 ci four."

In any case, with the T4 Miller was at the threshold of his breakthrough to greatness. ■

Miller T4, 1919

The T4 engine was Miller's first use of the twin-cam principle, and was conceived to fit the new three-liter, 183 ci formula. It used a barrel-type crankcase and cup cam followers. Light aluminum-alloy covers enclosed all engine accessories and presented a clean outer aspect. The T4 was drawn in full scale by Leo Goossen, his first important engineering-draftsman job. *FU*

Miller Factory, 1923
Posed in front of Miller's Long Beach
Avenue plant, from left, Ira Vail, Jimmy
Murphy, and visiting French racing driver
Antoine Mourré. A pretty collection of
mechanical jewelry. *GBC ex Art Streib Studio*

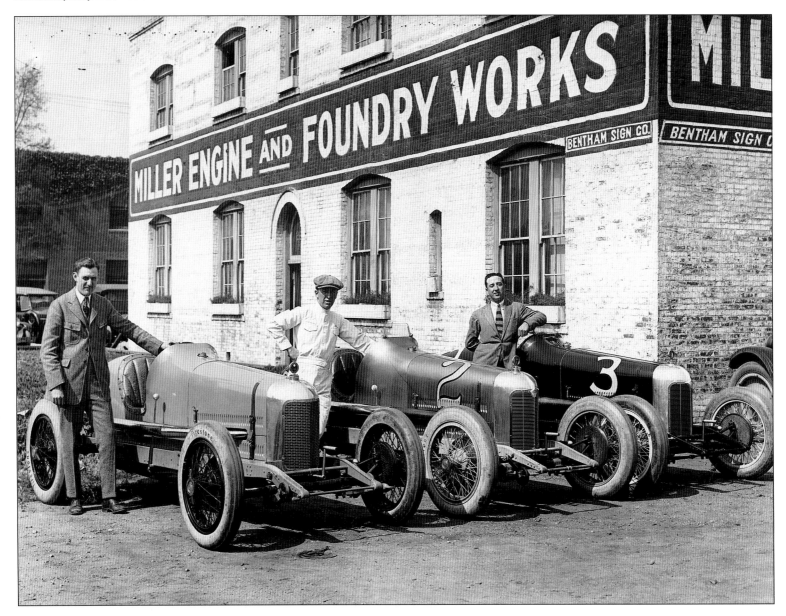

Chapter Five: **Miller at the Top**

Duesenberg, Le Mans, 1921
Jimmy Murphy, with riding mechanic Ernie Olson, won the French Grand Prix at Le Mans. After the successes of Ballot, limited as they were, this Duesenberg victory made a national vogue in the United States of the straight-eight principle. *GBC ex Ernie Olson*

O UT OF PATIENCE with the latest Miller engine, whichever it may have been, Cliff Durant had it replaced with one of the then-dominant Duesenberg eights. These were very worthy sources of power but, as history would have it, the particular specimen which Cliff received happened to be a lemon. It was so hopeless that, on the occasion of the Elgin, Illinois, Road Race on August 28, Cliff turned the car over to ace Tommy Milton and told him to keep it and do with it what he liked. Milton ran this rig at least until a race at Fresno on October 2, and always with frustrating results. It was not long after that last-straw experience that he ordered from Miller a new eight-cylinder. He was fond of claiming its authorship saying, modestly, "I'm the man who made Harry Miller." But everyone, and especially the contemporary press, testified that the first such engine had been ordered by Ira Vail. Milton granted that Vail had bought the first twin-cam 183. Vail himself told Fred Usher that he had ordered it from a Miller blueprint which inspired his confidence. It can be regarded as an eight-cylinder version of the T4, which reverted to the cam drive of the sohc four and the cast-iron integral-head block of the Peugeot, including the Burman-Peugeot innovations.

Other Miller activities toward the end of 1920 included the shipment by rail to Kansas City, Missouri of two engineless chassis. They were collected at the station and taken to the fine machine shop of W. W. Brown, where they were fitted with Brown-Brett-designed "all-aluminum" twin-cam sixes. They thus became the last of the Junior Specials. Both crashed at the Speedway the following May due to defective steering gears, which were not Miller-built.

On December 5, 1920, Cliff's father became a two-time loser in his struggle to control General Motors. He had seen this coming, and virtually overnight the new Durant Motor Company burst into being. By January 16, Cliff had severed all of his own ties with Chevrolet and GM in order to continue riding herd over his father's new operations in the West. Milton continued to campaign the Duesenberg-engined Durant Miller as a Chevrolet Special. He got it running well enough to finish second to

(above)

Miller Durant Special 183, 1922

Cliff Durant in his 183 Durant Special in which he would finish twelfth at Indy that year. *IMS*

(right)

Harry Miller and Group, 1922

Miller, far right, and his cohorts at Beverly Hills. From left, master mechanic Riley Brett, unidentified, Jimmy Murphy, Miller. *SM ex RB*

(far right)

Miller Leach Special, 1921

Thanksgiving Day race at Beverly Hills with Frank Elliott at the wheel of Ira Vail's primordial Miller 183. *GBC ex B. B. Korn*

(bottom right)

Durant Miller 183, 1921

Tommy Milton at the wheel of Cliff Durant's 183 on the Beverly Hills board speedway February 28, 1921. Behind the hand-brake lever it appears that the name "Chevrolet" had been hastily painted out. *FU*

(bottom far right)

Miller Leach Special, 1922

Frank Elliott and mechanic Herschel McKee in the Leach Special ready for the Indy 500, in which they would finish sixteenth. *IMS*

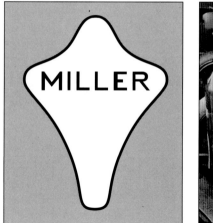

(far left)
Miller Emblem Blueprint, 1923
It was at this period that Leo Goossen designed the emblem that adorned many Miller radiators. It was cast in brass and nickel-plated. Leo redrew this from memory in the 1950s. *GBC ex LG*

(left)
Miller 183, 1922
Jimmy Murphy installed a Miller 183 (four carb throats only) engine in his Duesenberg, won the Indy 500 at all-time record speed, and went on to win the AAA National Championship. Miller was catapulted to international prominence overnight. *GBC ex Ernie Olson*

(below)
Miller 122, 1923
In the Italian Grand Prix at Monza, Jimmy Murphy finished the 800 km/500 miles about four minutes slower than the Fiats of Salamano and Nazzaro. They were pioneering supercharging; Murphy's third place Miller 122 was unblown. His mechanic, Ernie Olson, was checking an oil leak. *FU*

Leon Duray, circa 1924
Duray was one of the fastest and most spectacular drivers of the 1920s. Here he poses at Ascot in Los Angeles with World Heavyweight Boxing Champion Jack Dempsey. *GBC ex Leon Duray*

De Palma's Ballot in a 50-miler at Beverly Hills on February 28. But three weeks later the papers reported that the Miller plant was working around the clock on the Durant car. Obviously they were installing and fine-tuning its new Miller eight. Then on March 31 the papers reported that a new engine was being installed in Vail's car by Miller, and that it would run as a Leach Special.

It was at Fresno, on April 30, that the Miller

183 eight ran in competition for the first time, powering the Durant Miller Chevrolet Special to a mediocre finish. Milton left the car in Los Angeles and went to Indianapolis to accept a ride in one of Louis Chevrolet's Frontenacs. On the eve of the 500 the merger of the Miller Engine & Foundry Works with Leach Biltwell was announced. Harry Miller was named vice president of the new $5 million corporation, the intention of which was to manufacture "the only high-grade car built in the West." The

Miller eight in Vail's Leach Special had been completed only ten days before the still-unpainted car motored to a decent seventh place finish in what is still called the Memorial Day Classic.

Milton, the winner of the race, returned to Los Angeles at the end of June, "to work on the Miller." The engine had shown a tendency to warp valves, which Vail may have avoided by not going flat out. Milton, a very good practical engineer, determined that the cause of the problem was insufficient pressure within the cooling system, and he fixed it. He also availed himself of cam contours which had been developed by Colonel E. J. Hall for Fred Duesenberg. And then the new Miller 183 really began to wail.

Logically, Milton rechristened his borrowed car a Durant Special. His first race with the new camshaft grind and improved circulation of coolant was a 250-miler at Tacoma on the Fourth of July. He was the outright winner. His only other win during the last half of the year was in a sprint race at Phoenix on November 12. But on the 24th he was second in the 250-miler at Beverly Hills and, on December 11, second again in the inaugural race over the same distance at San Carlos, near San Francisco. The points he amassed made him AAA National Champion for 1921. The Durant Special earned the right to wear the numeral 1.

The Conquest of the Engine-Builder's Art

The 1922 season began with a 250-miler at Beverly Hills on March 5. Milton won it, establishing a whole set of new world records in the process. He and the new Miller 183 had become the hottest things on wheels. It was immediately following this race that Jimmy Murphy place an order with Miller for a 183 to be installed in the Duesenberg car with which he had won the French Grand Prix at Le Mans the previous July.

On April 2, Milton won another race at Beverly Hills, only to have the Durant Special outlawed by the AAA Contest Board, in a fit of truth-in-advertising righteousness over the naming of

Miller 122, 1925
This overhead view of National Champion Tommy Milton in his 122 clearly illustrates the car's extreme slimness and consequent aerodynamic effectiveness. European constructors took careful note. *GBC ex* Autocar

35

Duesenberg, 1924

The winning car in the 1924 Indy 500 was a Duesenberg driven by L. L. Corum and Joe Boyer. The mass of carburetor ram tubes made the car look like a Miller. *IMS*

Miller Durant Special 122, 1923

Cliff Durant bought a small fleet of 122s, one of which he drove into seventh place in the 1923 Indy 500. *IMS*

Miller 122, 1925

Harry Hartz finished fourth in the 1925 Indy 500, helped no doubt by the streamlining effect of aluminum wheel discs, as also used on the rear of Ralph De Palma's car. *GBC ex TW*

racing cars. Cliff, however, because his name was Durant, could not be denied the right to campaign this machine. So he repossessed it from Milton, while reimbursing his $6,000 investment in the engine. Thus prepared, Cliff filed his and the car's entry in the Indianapolis 500, less than two months away. Milton placed a rush order for a new Miller 183 engine and went to work on hustling together a car to go with it. It was no work of art, had cross-spring front suspension, and it ran as a Leach Special. Since Miller and Leach had merged, the Contest Board could not argue that its scruples of the moment were being violated.

On May 7, the 50-mile preliminary event on the Cotati boards was won by Pietro Bordino, at the wheel of a Fiat 804, the cream of European Grand Prix machines. Harry Miller was in Murphy's pit, assuring the tune of his new engine to a razor's edge. The 100-mile main event was won by the Miller-engined Murphy Special, on its first gallop, at an average of 115.34 mph. Bordino had averaged 114.50, and for only half that distance.

The conquest of the engine-builder's art which was announced at Beverly Hills in March and underlined at Cotati in May became accepted internationally at Indianapolis twenty-three days later, with Murphy's Miller-engined victory in the 500. The luckless Milton went out on the forty-fourth lap with chassis trouble which he contrived to blame on Miller. The Vail Leach, driven by Elliott, would have finished well, had it not been for axle failure on the 195th of the 200 laps. As for Cliff, who looked upon all this as recreational activity and not as a blood and/or money sport, had the pleasure of going the entire distance in fast company and of finishing a not-ignoble twelfth. Few people had an inkling of the role in this whole unfolding drama which had been played by Cliff Durant and his modest, much-thrashed and modified ex-Chevrolet Special.

Miller had been a local celebrity for years. With Murphy's victory at Indianapolis in 1922 Miller became a figure of international importance overnight. It was merely the beginning. ∎

Miller 122, 1925
The great Ralph De Palma finished his long and brilliant career at the wheel of a Miller 122, which he campaigned all over the country. *GBC ex TW*

Harry Miller, 1928
The maestro with his masterpiece, the last
91 engine on the dynamometer.
GBC ex Roy Richter

38

Chapter Six: **Miller Straight-Eight Anatomy**

Miller 122, 1923
Jimmy Murphy, now leader of the Durant team, with Harry Miller and the first of the 122s. *GBC ex Art Streib Studio*

VARIOUS AUTHORITIES, including Leo Goossen, have said that the Miller eight-cylinder 183 was a straightforward effort to combine the best features of the best racing engines of the day. Miller based much of his design concepts on the Ballot and the Duesenberg, both straight-eights.

The French Ballot, the most highly perfected racing engine in the world in the late 1910s and early 1920s, was the single-handed work of Ernest Henry of Switzerland, who had also engineered all of the classic GP Peugeots. The 1919 Ballot eight-cylinder 300 and Miller's eight-cylinder 183 of 1920 were, then, eight-cylinder derivatives of the prewar four-cylinder Peugeots—but with one difference. Henry had replaced the Peugeot's extravagantly complicated cam follower design with that of the exquisitely simple and direct cup type that Frenchman, Albert Morin, had patented during the war. These cup-type cam followers fitted over the valve stems and springs like tiny pistons, permitting the cams to attack the valve stems without wiping motion, but with all the efficient directness of the mushroom tappets in an L-head engine. It was a solution that, in time, would take over the automotive world.

To Miller's credit and benefit, he was there, practically when the breakthrough occurred. The last Henry Ballot had been produced, so it was Miller who kept the principle alive and transmitted it to others. Miller used it first in the T4, and it remained a hallmark of his practice henceforth. In the first two eight-cylinder 183s, as in the T4, he used flat-top cups, which were free to rotate in their bores.

As for the engines' top-end design, the successful American Duesenberg straight-eights made do with a single overhead camshaft driven by a vertical shaft and bevel gears at the front of the engine. This was a more economical solution than a train of spur gears, but it put all of the stress and wear on one pair of gear teeth at a time, at the top and bottom of the shaft. As the teeth wore, precision was lost in the opening and closing of the valves.

(right)
Duesenberg 183, 1920
Longitudinal section of the straight-eight 183 GP engine. As early as 1915, Duesenberg was manufacturing in series straight-eight marine engines for torpedo boats. *GBC ex* The Automobile Engineer, *London*

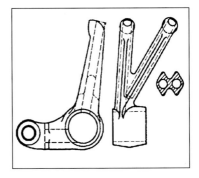

Duesenberg 183, 1920
The Duesenberg had three valves per cylinder, actuated by a single overhead camshaft and rockers. The two exhaust valves per cylinder were operated by a forked rocker, which was a weak point in the design.

GBC ex The Automobile Engineer, *London*

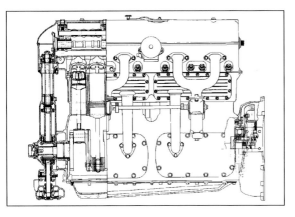

Miller's original plan for driving the dual camshafts was an exotic one—long connecting rods to drive the camshafts silently and positively. He and others would make a success of the system, but getting from conception to realization was difficult in this case. Thus, Miller seized upon the solution that he already knew so well—a train of ball-bearing-mounted spur gears. Miller used a wider contact area on his spur gears compared to Duesenberg's tiny bevel gears. With such a gear train, friction was nearly absent and if the workmanship was excellent, there was almost an absence of lost motion. Except for variations in valve-included angles, valve numbers, and combustion chamber shapes, this general engine architecture became another permanent hallmark of Miller practice.

Duesenberg had used three valves per cylinder, but instead of using paired inlet valves, as Bugatti did, Fred Duesenberg chose to pair his exhaust valves. He actuated them by means of a single, forked rocker arm, as Miller had done with his sohc fours. These tricky rockers proved to be a weak point in the Duesenberg design—raising the suspicion of compromise in the favor of reducing cost inherent in the concept.

Miller went all-out to outdo his competition. He continued to be faithful to employing four valves per cylinder in prism-shaped pent-roof combustion chambers in which the spark plugs were centered. As in the T4, he used dual overhead camshafts.

In the T4, he had also used the 60-degree valve-included angle of Ernest Henry practice but now, for his first eight-cylinder, he innovated. He narrowed the angle to 50 degrees, possibly under the influence of the astonishingly narrow 1920 Frontenac of some 35 degrees. It would be many decades before the advantages of narrow valve-included angles would become universally recognized.

The Ballots used a crankshaft that ran in five main bearings mounted in a barrel-type crankcase. The three intermediate mains were carried in babbitted bronze diaphragms that gave solid 360-degree support; this was typical Henry practice, which Miller knew so well. The Duesenbergs used a crankcase that was split below the crankshaft centerline. Their cases were a semi-barrel type, in that the crankshafts had to be inserted horizontally, from the rear, main-bearing support being around 220 degrees. And Duesenberg made do with just three main bearings, the rearmost being a ball race. Since that seemed to work well enough for Duesenberg, Miller adopted the principle, putting an identical shaft in a Henry-type case, with a central diaphragm main bearing. The barrel case with internal diaphragms became another Miller hallmark.

Duesenberg used a single iron eight-cylinder block cast integrally with the upper half of the crankcase. Miller, however, returned to the Henry practice of his Peugeot days, using two cast-iron blocks in groups of four cylinders. The blocks were shaped so that they could be machined from all sides; their sides were left wide open to be covered, after machining, with aluminum plates, which completed the water jacketing. This technique made for the most accurate control of core location during the casting process.

In the first two Miller eight-cylinder 183 engines, the spark plug bosses were of the conventional type: integral elements of the block and head casting. In subsequent production, however, a hole was left that corresponded to each spark plug and through which casting cores could also be controlled. After machining, these holes received spark plug bosses that were in the form of machined steel cups, which threaded into the combustion chambers and were sealed at the top by

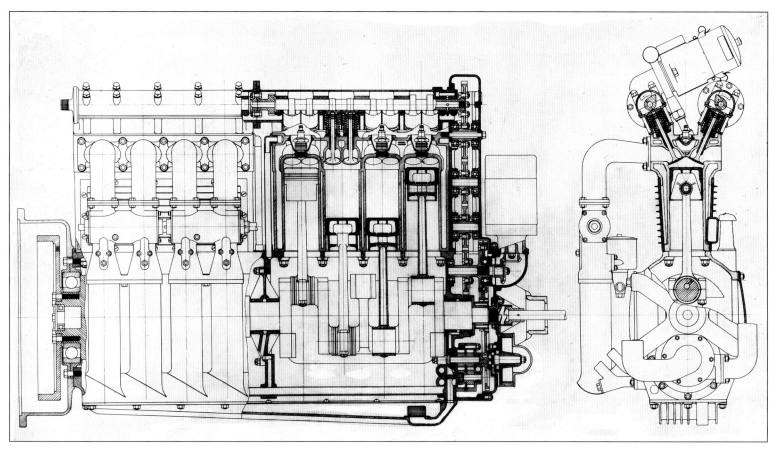

Miller 183, 1921
Leo Goossen's first really great drafting—
and engineering—project: drawing, in ink,
the definitive Miller 183 in longitudinal and
transverse sections. *GBC ex LG*

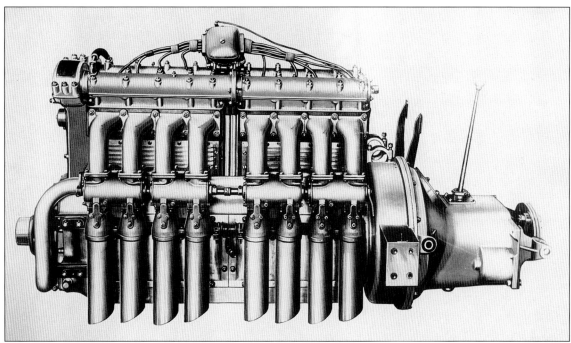

Miller 183, 1921
More Goossen handiwork: the inlet side of
the 183. Miller had developed twin-throat
carburetors during World War I, and used
them here to give each cylinder a complete
respiratory tract of its own. With this, plus
twin cams and four valves per cylinder, the
Duesenberg engine became obsolete
overnight. *GBC ex LG*

(above)
Miller 183, 1923
Those who could not afford the new 122 engines destroked the old 183, this being Harlan Fengler's Indy entry for 1923. *IMS*

(above right)
Miller 122, 1924
The 122 engine in its pure state. Esthetic impact was as important to Miller as was performance. *IMS*

Miller 122, 1923
Murphy's Durant Miller 122 in the IMS garage area. Murphy qualified it fifth and finished in third. *IMS*

rubber rings. This technique insured that all plugs were uniformly separated from water by a mere 1/16 in of metal. And it permitted the production of cylinder blocks that of the utmost precision. Small wonder that Bugatti, beginning in 1930, adopted both technique and design with perfect fidelity. These spark plug cups became another permanent Miller hallmark.

A particularly elegant touch that began with the eight-cylinder 183 was the near-invisible means of anchoring the iron blocks to the light aluminum-alloy case. This was achieved by steel studs in the bottoms of the blocks, the studs registering with holes in the upper flange of the crankcase and projecting to its interior. Nuts and lock washers, torqued up from inside the case, completed the fastening. The final aesthetic result was wonderful even though, from the structural standpoint, this solution left much to be desired. All of these features of the classic Miller block lived on—even to the end of the Offenhauser engine line. So did the front engine-mount spider, a characteristic Miller object made of cast bronze, suitably ground and polished.

Miller also innovated with several other features in his eight-cylinder 183. The engines did not have siamesed cylinders; water circulated freely around them all. Duesenberg used the new Delco system of ignition fired by battery and distributor; Miller did likewise at the beginning, even including an electric generator among his engine's accessories. After first dispensing with the generator and relying upon the battery alone for spark, all this complication and weight soon gave way to a simple Robert Bosch magneto.

Duesenberg used a dry oil sump as well as

Miller 91, 1926
The first 91 engine: The two nickel-plated water manifolds are tapered like musical instruments; according to the amount of liquid to be passed. Bugatti adopted this practice after he had acquired his pair of 91s.
GBC ex LG

Miller 91, 1926
Goossen drew the 91, but everyone in the plant, from Miller to the janitor, took pride in the esthetic perfection of its products. Miller and his crew would build about thirty-five 91 engines, permitting a high degree of development and refinement to take place. *GBC ex LG*

tubular-section connecting rods, both of which were already Miller practice and remained so. Interestingly, whereas Duesenberg used a traditional stroke-to-bore ratio of 1.85:1, Miller opted for a modern-for-the-times ratio of 1.49:1. Miller experimented with detachable cylinder heads on his first two eight-cylinder 183s, but quickly converted to casting them integrally with the blocks.

From the beginning, Miller tested carburetors with two, four, or eight throats. The four- and eight-throat arrangements became standard, depending upon individual preference and tuning. And from the start, Miller and his team experimented with ram tuning of induction systems, using a stopwatch and cut-and-try methods at the Beverly Hills board track. The team determined optimum inlet stack lengths and learned to bevel the stack ends and to turn their openings away from the direction of travel as the pressure of forward motion seemed to perturb air intake.

The Duesenberg engine used a 4-4 crankshaft, as opposed to a 2-4-2. Crankshaft counterweights were new and exotic, and Duesenberg was not tempted to try them. Miller, having copied the Duesenberg crankshaft exactly, found his crankshafts breaking with predictable regularity. The situation remained desperate until Frank Elliott's brother Clarence intervened. He was a mathematics instructor at Cal Tech, with a strong interest in mechanical engineering, and he designed a counterbalanced shaft for the eight-cylinder 183 as well as persuading Miller of the importance of heat-treating such parts. This put an end to the crankshaft crisis.

What Miller had not been able to study were the cam contours that determined the valve timing of the current Duesenbergs and were a key to their performance. These contours had been conceived by E. J. Hall specifically for Fred Duesenberg. The first purchasers of Miller eight-cylinder 183s—Ira Vail and Tommy Milton—found their new engines to be lifeless, and Milton deduced that it was Miller's cam contours that were at fault. In an epic stroke of industrial espionage in American racing history, ex-Duesenberg team man Milton

used his old inside contacts to dislodge a print of the new Hall cams. The designs were so radical compared with contemporary racing practice that Milton could not believe his eyes. But Miller tried them, and they proved to be the major turning point in the development of the eight-cylinder 183 engine, as well as an important one in Miller's personal career. From that point onward, the Miller legend only continued to grow.

The Showmanship of Racing

In 1921, as soon as the eight-cylinder 183 was sorted out, Miller began constructing complete racing cars in which to mount the engine. The cars' wagon-sprung suspension systems were merely

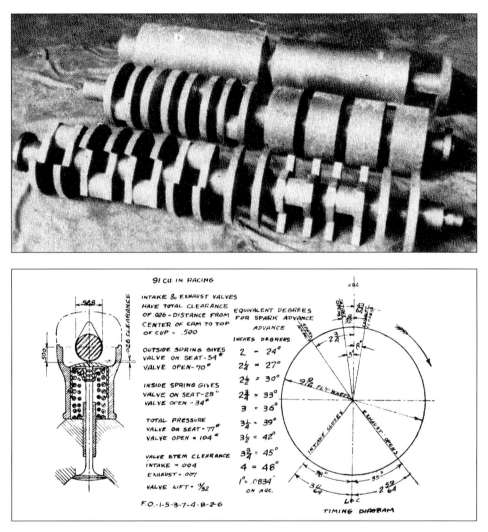

Miller 91, 1926
The valve timing data sheet supplied by Miller with the 91 engine. Most owners would experiment with other cam grinds, in search of a more advantageous combination. *GBC ex LG*

(*top*)
Miller Crankshaft, mid-1920s
Stages in the machining of a Miller crankshaft from a solid steel billet, as presented in a Miller catalog of the time. *GBC*

refined versions of standard touring-car practice, but this happened to be the best answer to the requirements of oval-track racing, regardless of the surface. In fact, there were competitive cars running at Indianapolis in the fifties with suspension systems and running gear that differed from the old Millers only in the size of their wheels, rims, and tires.

In order to exert the most rigid control over the balance between the strength and the lightness of parts, Miller broke with the established practice of adapting production-car components to race-car use. Practically every part of every Miller car was always made in his own plant. All nonferrous castings were made in the factory's own foundry and only the cylinder blocks were cast elsewhere. All machining and sheet-metal work was done on the premises—even the flawless frame channels were hammered out of flat sheet stock by hand. Miller purchased the rims for his wheels but, learning from the failures of others, machined from forged billets his own splined Rudge-type hubs. He made his own axles, steering linkages, steering gearboxes, clutches, transmissions, gears, crankshafts, and shock absorbers; only such obvious items as magnetos and instruments were purchased.

For every part, an engineering drawing existed. And Miller used the finest materials available. All stressed steel parts were machined from strong but ductile 6145 chrome-vanadium alloy; he used mild steel only for his frame rails, where it was the best choice. In addition he pioneered the racing use of chrome-molybdenum, which he employed in his axle tubes.

The importance of esthetic effect was of fundamental importance to Harry Miller. "Miller could have made a lot more money if he hadn't cared so much about finish," Fred Offenhauser explained. "But he didn't think that way. He didn't want to see machining or file marks on metal. All his castings had to be hand-scraped and polished to a satin finish after every part was machined. It took us from 6,000 to 6,500 man-hours to build a complete car in the twenties. About half that time went into engine, clutch, and transmission; the balance into frame, running gear, and body. Between 700 and 1,000 hours went into beautifying—just putting the finish on each machine. Showmanship is a big part of racing, and Harry's cars made every race a show to remember."

Racing was a business devoted deliberately to the creation of absolutely superior competition machines that were, at one and the same time, works of art. This meant that one had to seek out, attract, and engage exceptional talent in each of the disciplines involved. This Miller did, creating a sort of American Bauhaus of the Machine. And this was Harry Miller's most remarkable creation of all. ■

Miller 91, 1928
The 91 engine on display in the Indianapolis Motor Speedway Museum. It is an example of how individual owners would modify the basic product in search of performance advantage. *GB*

(far right)
Miller 91, 1928
This display engine in the Indianapolis Museum is that of the 1928 Boyle Valve Special, with high-surface intercooler of that team's design. *GB*

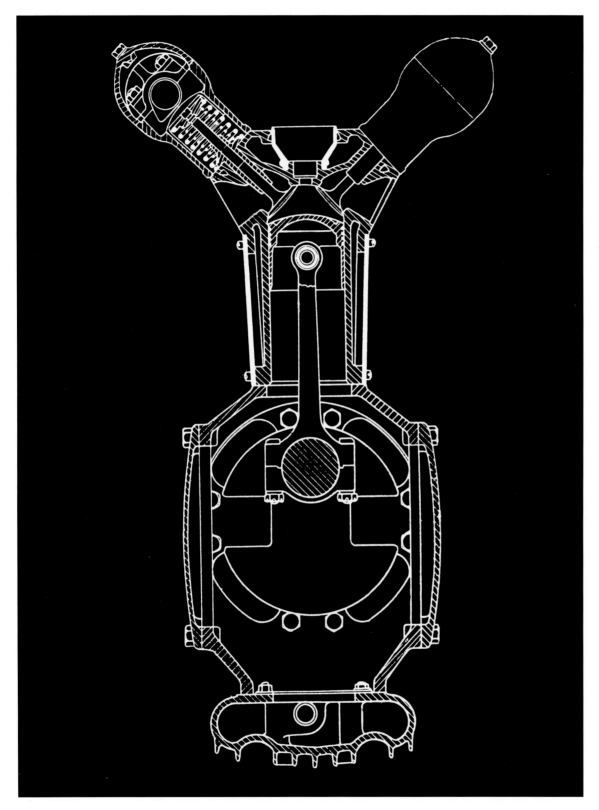

Miller 91, 1927
In 1927, race driver and entrepreneur Earl Cooper, as the Cooper Engineering Company, produced a team of cars that were copies of the Miller 91 product, but with certain modifications. This was a Cooper drawing of the 91 engine. All was normal Miller technique except the cam covers, which have a different cross section. *GBC ex Automotive Industries*

Miller Special, 1926

Rookie Frank Lockhart won the 1926 Indy 500 at 95.885 mph, faster than he had qualified the ivory-white 91 owned by driver Pete Kreis. It was an astonishing exploit in a short career that was filled with them. *IMS*

Chapter Seven: The Golden Age of Harry Miller

T
HE YEARS BETWEEN 1919 and 1929 were the golden age of the thoroughbred American racing car. Its harbingers included the twin-cam Frontenacs, which had been gestating since 1915, and the six-cylinder Richards Special, an Ernest Henry derivative via Sunbeam. There was Miller's single-cam four, which was a giant if faltering step in the right direction. And then there was Henry's own straight-eight Ballot, designed specifically for Indianapolis by the master of the art and it was the ideal to which to aspire.

In 1920, Duesenberg adopted eight cylinders in line and stepped up from walking beam to a single overhead camshaft. Miller advanced to his dohc T4, but it remained stillborn. Then came 1921 and the great Frontenac twin-cam straight-eight. It held vast promise for the future, but it lacked a Cliff Durant. That patron of the sport chose to put his money on Harry Miller and his new eight-cylinder 183. With a few critical modifications to the two original prototypes, classic Miller engine architecture was permanently defined. The golden age had begun and only similar thoroughbreds were competitive. Duesenberg, the other great contemporary force in American automobile racing at the time, had to adopt Miller design principles in order to survive in the same world.

Miller's domination of the sport began with Jimmy Murphy's victory at Indianapolis in 1922. From this breakthrough, Miller almost overwhelmingly reigned at The Brickyard throughout the 1920s. In the years 1922–1929, Millers won five 500s and typically placed at least six cars in the top ten. It was an enviable record.

Birth of the Miller 122

About a dozen Miller eight-cylinder 183s were built before the expiration of the 183 ci displacement formula at the end of 1922. A two-liter, 122 ci formula was enacted, and in the summer of 1922, Miller began the design of a new engine and car for the class. The basic design of the 183 did not leave a great deal to be desired, but there were some important changes made for the new 122 nonetheless. For one, a proper five-

Culver City Boardtrack, circa 1925
A fantastic story-telling photo of the Culver City board speedway: the movie sets and pre-sound stages that press against the wooden saucer; the density of the crowd; the ability of grandstand spectators to observe the entire theater of operations.
Dick Wallen/Philip Harms

Miller & Duesenberg at the Indianapolis 500, 1922–1929		
Year Winner	**Cars(engines) in the Top Ten**	
	Miller	**Duesenberg**
1922 Miller	1	7
1923 Miller	6	1
1924 Duesenberg	8	2
1925 Duesenberg	6	3
1926 Miller	9	1
1927 Duesenberg	8	2
1928 Miller	9	1
1929 Miller	7	2

Record Certificate, 1926
AAA Record Certificate issued to Leon Duray for setting the class and absolute record driving his Miller for 250 miles at 136.05 mph. *GBC ex Leon Duray*

the idea came to Miller via Milton from Colonel E. J. Hall, a recurring presence in American engine engineering history. However, FIAT engineer Giulio Cesare Cappa had introduced the principle on his firm's Tipo 402 and 403 racing cars in 1921. And they had been clamorously successful, as would be the similarly endowed 1923 Fiat 405 GP car.

The stroke to bore ratio of the new Miller 122 was within a hair of being identical to Fiat's new Grand Prix champion-to-be. And, finally, Miller abandoned the narrow, 50-degree valve-included angle of the eight-cylinder 183 in favor of an Italianesque 98 degrees. The Fiat 405 went overboard with 104 degrees—a record for all time.

These were the significant changes that marked the Miller 122. The new engine was created primarily by scaling down and refining its excellent predecessor. Delco ignition was retained, although a Bosch magneto conversion became available in 1924.

The bodies of the eight-cylinder 183s had been remarkably narrow, but those of the 122s seemed to be more so, the drawings calling for a maximum width of 18 in, within which the driver's hips were expected to fit. Aerodynamically, they were slippery projectiles, as the record list confirmed.

Miller was fond of gun-blued steel and blued his connecting rods to protect their satin surface. Now he began bluing all the bright parts of his cars: axles, radiator shells, and so on. Clients who preferred the gleam of nickel could do their own plating, and many did. The cars were astonishing jewels, as Mark Dees noted in *The Miller Dynasty*: "The wonderful Miller 122 was the first pure racing car to be series produced, but in reviewing the thousands of working drawings for these machines, one is constantly impressed with the immense artistry and thought given to each detail. Nearly every stressed part: gear, shaft, bolt, clevis, and stud was specially machined from chrome-vanadium steel stock to the precise dimensions required, unless they were massive enough to be cast in bronze or aluminum."

main-bearing crankshaft was created to replace the existing three-main-bearing type. Another change, and a radical one, was the adoption of just two valves per cylinder, permitting the use of perfectly hemispheric combustion chambers. Among their advantages were an optimum surface-to-volume ratio, minimum heat rejection to coolant, and the possibility of easily machining the volume of each chamber, all to an identical degree.

Miller's 122 was America's first use of truly hemispheric chambers in connection with dual overhead camshafts. Leo Goossen believed that

Miller Special, 1926
Frank Lockhart's wife was part of the family enterprise, the simple object of which was to render Frank the fastest man on earth. He was a self-taught mechanical genius who hired good engineers as soon as he could afford them. *GBC ex Carrie Lockhart*

Miller 91, 1927
With his 91 engine pulling 285 bhp, on April 11, 1927, at Muroc Dry Lake in Southern California, Lockhart set an incredible 171 mph record one way, and averaged 164 over the two-way measured mile, timed by AAA Contest Board officials. *GBC ex Carrie Lockhart*

Lockhart Miller LSR, 1928
The U-16 Lockhart land speed record chassis, made up of two Miller 91 engines. The finned objects above were supercharger intercoolers.
GBC ex Zenas Weizel

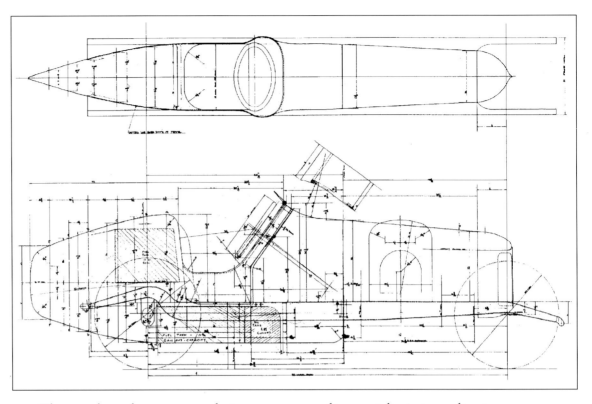

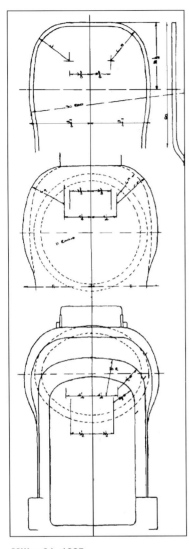

Miller 91, 1925
Leo Goossen's drawings for the standard 91 frame and body, pinnacles of the Golden Age. The body weighed 76 lb. *Mark L. Dees*

The number of 122 cars made is uncertain, but fifteen is a fair approximation—and it was certainly enough for the series to become highly perfected. Goossen estimated that between twenty-five and thirty engines were made, some of these being for replacement and some perhaps for installation in racing hydroplanes.

The Development of Superchargers

Early specimens of the Miller 122s developed around 120 bhp at 5000 rpm and weighed about 303 lb. The cars were wonderfully fast, given the power output.

Then, at Indianapolis in 1924, Duesenberg had the immortal distinction of introducing centrifugal supercharging—forced induction by means of a gear-driven compressor. There, at the dawn of its development, the supercharger probably contributed little to a Duesenberg victory, however it announced to all the world that a breakthrough had taken place, and it took carburetion expert Harry Miller no time at all to become an out-

standing specialist in its application.

Since the 122 engine had been designed without a power takeoff for this purpose in mind, one had to be improvised. The solution consisted of a $1,200 bolt-on kit with a supercharger that was gear-driven by the aft ends of the two camshafts. It brought the engine's weight up to about 340 lb. It also raised output to an easily accessible 203 bhp at 5800 rpm, with as much as 235 bhp being reported by some of the tuners.

The two-liter formula had been adopted internationally as a means for reducing speeds and making racing safer. As such it had failed in a spectacular manner, and a new dose of the same medicine was prescribed by the governing bodies of the sport.

The Miller 91 is Born

As the roof was blown off the 122 ci, two-liter formula by the development of supercharging, a new formula was inaugurated. Between the years 1926–1929, piston displacement in international competition, including the United States, would be 1500 cc, 1.5 liters, 91.5 ci. Miller responded with his 91 engine, a creation that would soon become immortal in racing history.

The 122 was a refined 183, and the 91 was a 122, refined still further. The Miller 91 was based on a bore and stroke of 2.1875x3.00 in, which gave the engine a displacement of 90.2 ci, 1476 cc. Because of the tiny size of its individual parts and because of its displacement, it was commonly spoken of as "a little engine." In reality, it was perhaps the longest 1.5 liter engine ever made.

The 91 was one of Miller's finest works of art. Although it was derived directly from the 122, the process involved much engineering. From the start, Miller chose to incorporate a supercharger into this new design.

This little engine started out in life in 1926 and was credited with an output of 154 bhp at 7000 rpm. No one knew much about fuels at the time, and this figure no doubt was obtained using the usual combination of good gasoline, a splash of benzol, and a trace amount of tetraethyl lead. Driver and car owner Leon Duray began experiments at the Miller plant using methanol, or wood alcohol, as fuel. His tests had astounding results: he found it difficult to discover the limit of an engine's ability to ingest, burn, and convert methanol into kinetic energy.

The Miller 91 seemed to be infinitely responsive to the tuner's art. Or perhaps it was just that this whole panoply of technologies came together at this one point in history. The results were mind-boggling figures for the time, whether they be of specific fuel consumption, supercharger pressures, elapsed time over a given distance, power per unit of displacement, or just plain absolute speed.

Lockhart Miller LSR, 1928
The Lockhart "beach car" reached 220 mph at Daytona before crashing. *GBC ex Zenas Weizel*

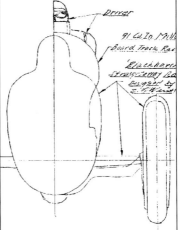

(right)

Miller Catalog, 1927

The catalog was modest, listing only some of the numerous 91 and 122 records.

GBC ex Floyd Clymer

(above)

Lockhart Miller LSR, 1927

Lockhart was within reach of the LSR. This drawing by one of Lockhart's engineers, Zenas Weizel of Cal Tech, shows the frontal outlines of the standard 91 rear-drive and of a projected machine for attacking the LSR. *GBC ex Zenas Weizel*

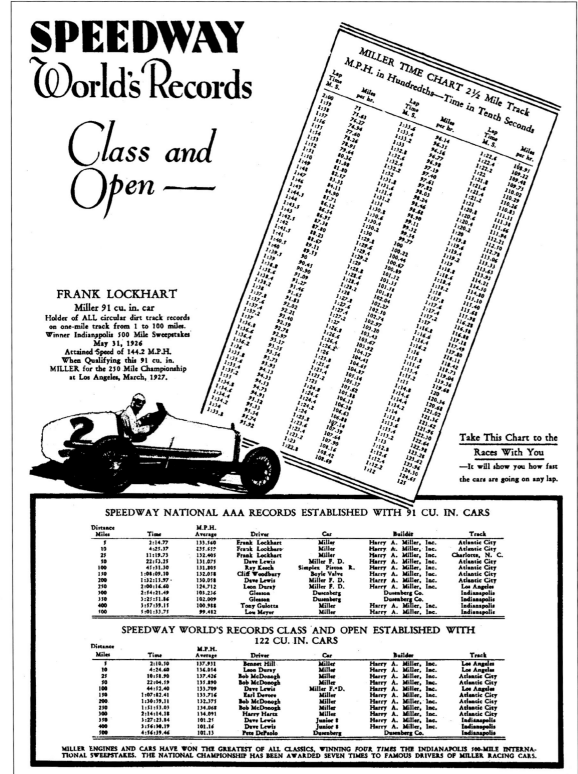

SPEEDWAY
World's Records
Class and Open —

FRANK LOCKHART

Miller 91 cu. in. car
Holder of ALL circular dirt track records
on one-mile track from 1 to 100 miles.
Winner Indianapolis 500 Mile Sweepstakes
May 31, 1926
Attained Speed of 144.2 M.P.H.
When Qualifying this 91 cu. in.
MILLER for the 250 Mile Championship
at Los Angeles, March, 1927.

Take This Chart to the Races With You

—It will show you how fast the cars are going on any lap.

SPEEDWAY NATIONAL AAA RECORDS ESTABLISHED WITH 91 CU. IN. CARS

Distance Miles	Time	M.P.H. Average	Driver	Car	Builder	Track
5	2:14.77	133.560	Frank Lockhart	Miller	Harry A. Miller, Inc.	Atlantic City
10	4:25.37	135.652	Frank Lockhart	Miller	Harry A. Miller, Inc.	Atlantic City
25	11:19.73	132.405	Frank Lockhart	Miller	Harry A. Miller, Inc.	Charlotte, N. C.
50	22:53.25	131.075	Dave Lewis	Miller F. D.	Harry A. Miller, Inc.	Atlantic City
100	45:31.30	131.805	Ray Keech	Simplex Piston R.	Harry A. Miller, Inc.	Atlantic City
150	1:08:09.10	132.058	Cliff Woodbury	Boyle Valve	Harry A. Miller, Inc.	Atlantic City
200	1:32:15.97	130.058	Dave Lewis	Miller F. D.	Harry A. Miller, Inc.	Atlantic City
250	2:00:14.60	124.712	Leon Duray	Miller F. D.	Harry A. Miller, Inc.	Los Angeles
300	2:54:21.49	103.236	Gleason	Dusenberg	Dusenberg Co.	Indianapolis
350	3:25:51.86	102.009	Gleason	Dusenberg	Dusenberg Co.	Indianapolis
400	3:57:39.15	100.988	Tony Gulotta	Miller	Harry A. Miller, Inc.	Indianapolis
500	5:01:33.75	99.482	Lou Meyer	Miller	Harry A. Miller, Inc.	Indianapolis

SPEEDWAY WORLD'S RECORDS CLASS AND OPEN ESTABLISHED WITH 122 CU. IN. CARS

Distance Miles	Time	M.P.H. Average	Driver	Car	Builder	Track
5	2:10.50	137.931	Bennet Hill	Miller	Harry A. Miller, Inc.	Los Angeles
10	4:24.60	136.054	Leon Duray	Miller	Harry A. Miller, Inc.	Los Angeles
25	10:58.90	137.426	Bob McDonogh	Miller	Harry A. Miller, Inc.	Atlantic City
50	22:04.59	135.890	Bob McDonogh	Miller	Harry A. Miller, Inc.	Atlantic City
100	44:52.40	133.709	Dave Lewis	Miller F. D.	Harry A. Miller, Inc.	Los Angeles
150	1:07:82.41	133.716	Earl Devore	Miller	Harry A. Miller, Inc.	Atlantic City
200	1:30:39.11	132.375	Bob McDonogh	Miller	Harry A. Miller, Inc.	Atlantic City
250	1:51:53.03	134.068	Bob McDonogh	Miller	Harry A. Miller, Inc.	Atlantic City
300	2:14:14.18	134.091	Harry Hartz	Miller	Harry A. Miller, Inc.	Atlantic City
350	3:27:23.84	101.25	Dave Lewis	Junior 8	Harry A. Miller, Inc.	Indianapolis
400	3:56:30.19	101.16	Dave Lewis	Junior 8	Harry A. Miller, Inc.	Indianapolis
500	4:56:39.46	101.13	Pete DePaolo	Dusenberg	Dusenberg Co.	Indianapolis

MILLER ENGINES AND CARS HAVE WON THE GREATEST OF ALL CLASSICS, WINNING *FOUR TIMES* THE INDIANAPOLIS 500-MILE INTERNATIONAL SWEEPSTAKES. THE NATIONAL CHAMPIONSHIP HAS BEEN AWARDED SEVEN TIMES TO FAMOUS DRIVERS OF MILLER RACING CARS.

For example, Roland Bugatti recalled that on the Bugatti dynamometer, Miller 91s could be counted on to pull a *steady* 200 bhp at around 8000 rpm. Bugatti had created a faithful copy of the Miller 91 engine, from the top of the crankcase on up, but the 200 bhp output was when the engine was in rather *ordinary* tune. Asked how much horsepower he got from his 91s, Leon Duray would answer, "Anything you want." It all depended upon how you chose to set the engine up: for qualifying, sprints, record-breaking, or endurance. Duray did them all. When Frank Lockhart drove his tiny 91 to an officially timed 164 mph on California's Muroc Dry Lake in 1927, it took about 285 bhp for him to attain that speed. He did 171 mph in one direction, at a time when the World Land Speed Record stood at 203.79 mph, set by a specialized record machine of locomotive proportions. When Tommy Milton and C. W. van Ranst built the 91-based Detroit Special for Cliff Durant during the same period, they introduced two-stage supercharging and achieved some 300 bhp.

From the standpoint of sheer performance, the spectacle on the speedways around the country was utterly fantastic; brilliant new records were set everywhere. Most of those for the longer dis-

tances were not just displacement-class records but absolute ones, such as Meyer's 99.4 mph for 500 miles, Duray's 124.7 for 250, Keech's 131.8 for 100, and Duray's 148.1 mph for 2.5 miles. Running on the old brick surface with inherently slow corners, Duray's 1928 Indianapolis lap record of 124.018 mph remained unbroken until 1937, the longest a qualifying record has stood in the track's history.

To meet the needs of both boat and auto racing, perhaps as many as fifty 91 engines were made. Along with their brilliance they were doggedly reliable. And, as brilliant as the racing was, it became downright boring. Almost everyone ran so steadily that there was no traffic, no changing of positions—just processions.

These parades of Miller 91-powered cars around racetracks from coast to coast were one of the chief factors that brought the golden age of American thoroughbred race cars to an end. Other factors included the expiration of the 91.5 ci formula and the Great Depression, which struck at the same moment. Another factor was the decay of the magnificent board speedways that used to dot the nation, which was due mainly to the effects of weather.

An era had ended, but what a glorious piece of our patrimony that epoch was. ■

(above)
Miller Special, 1927
Louis Meyer qualified his gold and black 91 rear-drive at 111.352 mph and won the 1927 Indy 500 with an average of 99.482. Standing were Louis' father, Pop Meyer, and his sponsor, Alden Sampson II. *IMS*

(left)
Miller Special, 1928
On his way to becoming Indy's first three-time winner, Meyer qualified his rear-drive 91 at 114.704 mph and finished second to Billy Arnold in the Miller-Hartz entry. Master mechanic/engineer Riley Brett was at center and Pop Meyer next to his son.
SM ex RB

Miller 122 Front-Drive, 1925
Bennett Hill, a graduate engineer who
drove for Miller, strikes a pose of utter
hopelessness after trying out the first 122
front-wheel-drive car at Indy. *GBC ex IMS*

13th Annual 500 Mile Race
Indianapolis Motor Speedway
MAY-30-th 1925.
BENNETT HILL IN MILLER SPECIAL.

Photo # 9208
KIRKPATRICK
629. W. WASH. St.
Indianapolis, Ind.
1925

Chapter Eight: **Miller Front-Wheel Drive**

Miller 91 Front-Drives, 1928
The front-wheel-drive Millers were terrific performers. In this starting lineup at Altoona, six of the fourteen starters were front-wheel-drives, the first two rows consisting solely of them. *Joseph Freeman*

"THE HOLY GRAIL OF AMERICAN racing machinery," are museum-owner Miles Collier's words for it, and for those of us who lived all or part of the Miller experience, they fit very well. There was something about his cars that was close to being sublime. Looking at them, imperfection was the farthest thing from one's mind. They seemed to be a perfectly integrated, harmonious whole, as machines and as sculptural objects. If Harry Miller had done nothing more in his highly creative career than give the world front-wheel-drive as a practical reality, his significant place in history would be assured.

How this all came to be I first learned from Leo Goossen's lips, and that is the interpretation of history that I recounted in *The Golden Age of the American Racing Car* in 1966. Jimmy Murphy, having won practically everything, found himself in a position to commission the creation of a new machine, something uniquely superior to all the rest. His mechanic, Riley Brett—Goossen continued—suggested front-wheel-drive, praising its theoretical advantages. Murphy liked the idea and asked Miller what he could do. Miller studied the question and came back with a proposal for a machine with a transverse engine, located ahead of the car's front axle. Murphy rejected this approach because it would not leave room for a straight-eight engine, the winning combination then, and for years to come. Miller and Goossen then sketched a straight-eight with its flywheel end forward between the frame rails, with clutch, conventional transmission and final drive ahead of it. The trouble with this enormously long power train was that it pushed the center of gravity so far aft that there would be insufficient weight on the front tires, to give them traction and bite. At that juncture, Goossen said, Miller proposed a compact, transverse transmission with built-in final-drive gears—we call it a transaxle now. The space would be cramped and the gears therefore narrow and a bit delicate. Also, the transmission would have to be after the ring and pinion gears instead of before, as in standard practice. Murphy bought the idea and Leo got to figure it all out on the drawing board. "I don't know how I ever did it,"

Miller Patent Drawing, 1927

Miller's patent for a system of driving the front wheels of a motor vehicle had been forgotten until found by car historian Richard Fabris in the early 1960s.

GBC ex Richard Fabris

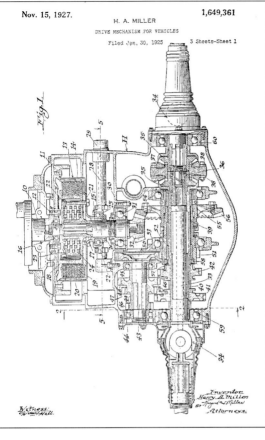

Miller Drawing, 1925

Leo Goossen made this drawing for the author in 1965, copied from an original Miller blueprint dated July 1925. It establishes the outboard-brake car as the first in the front-drive series. Only one of this type was made. *GBC ex LG*

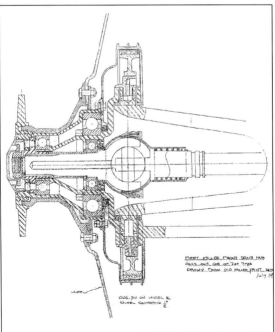

he said. Warning me that Riley Brett took credit for the idea, he said that I should interview him anyway. That was in the mid-fifties and Brett, a notoriously difficult personality, was not receiving me at the time.

The next breakthrough in this story came in 1961, when Auburn-Cord-Duesenberg historian Richard Fabris happened to discover us Patent 1,649,361, in the name of Harry A. Miller, for a "Drive Mechanism for Vehicles." The application had been filed on January 30, 1925, and it was for the awesomely intricate "front drive unit" that Leo said that he, Leo, had engineered. It would work at either end of a vehicle, and the text made radiant claims for its virtues. The text covers only the transaxle, not even the inboard brakes. I sent a copy of the patent to Leo, who expressed shock that Miller would have done this without his knowledge. I wrote the story his way and it became part of the published literature.

In Manhattan in 1978, I spent an afternoon with Miller's son, Ted. I had recently learned from the Rosen Papers that Brett, instead of being—along with Ernie Olson—simply "Murphy's mechanic," in reality had been an important person on Miller's payroll. "That's true," Ted said. "He was a very competent engineer."

In Los Angeles a few days later, I gave Brett a call. One of the grand old men of his calling, he still held court in the office of his huge machine shop, where much history had been hatched. At age 83, he was bright and chipper as a bird. Receiving me warmly, he told me categorically that it was not he who had proposed front-wheel-drive to Murphy, but Miller himself. He said that he never had liked front-wheel-drive, and never had seen any advantage to it other than the elimination of the conventional driveshaft and much unsprung weight on the rear axle. The one idea which originated with him, he still stressed, was that of the transverse front-drive unit. He did not comment upon the fact that Miller had patented a certain interpretation of that idea.

Brett confirmed that he had indeed worked for Ben F. Gregory in Kansas City who, three or

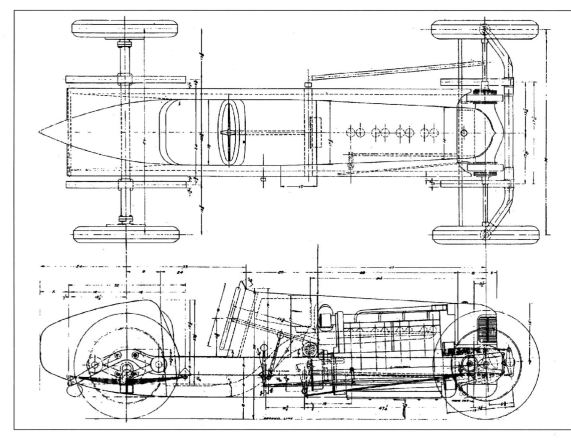

Miller 122 Front-Drive, 1924
Original assembly layout drawing for the Miller 122 front-wheel-drive, a superb blending of art and machine. It was drawn for Miller by the brother of Frank Elliott, Cal Tech mathematics professor Clarence V. Elliott. He also designed the counterbalanced crankshaft for the 183.
Mark L. Dees

four years before Miller, had built a few front-wheel-drive racing and passenger cars, with turned-around engines and De Dion front axles. That was pure coincidence, Riley said, and, as far as he knew, it had nothing to do with what Miller suggested to Murphy.

I asked Riley what he thought of the possible role of the Frontmobile of Camden, New Jersey, which, in 1916, used a reversed engine, combined with a transverse front drive unit and De Dion axle. The chassis, startlingly suggestive of the Miller solution, had been well covered in the automotive press at the time. There was still one of the cars in the Harrah Collection in Reno in 1978. All this came as new news to Riley Brett.

Another notable element in the folklore of front-wheel-drive is to be found in *The Los Angeles Examiner* for February 27, 1916. Therein an article describes how the famous front-wheel-drive Christie, generally conceded to be the fastest sprint car in the world, had just left the Miller shop after having undergone thorough revision. The car had been using Miller carburetors for at least two years. Miller must have had a fair knowledge of the Christie transverse-engine approach to front-wheel-drive.

As Goossen told the story, he and Miller were the lone authors of the Miller front-wheel-drive. Miller, intuitive genius, created most of the ideas. Goossen, young, gifted, shy engineer, made them work. Although the patented transaxle was the key to making the Miller front-wheel-drive work, no one ever told me that, at that precise period, Miller's world was almost completely subjugated to exotic transmissions and their large-scale commercialization. The Rosen Papers are replete with the documented details. Here we have the space only to summarize, but readers seeking much more detailed treatment will find it in my article, "Fresh Footnotes to Miller Front Drive" in *Automobile Quarterly* Volume 21, Number 4 1983.

Cord Patent Drawing, 1932

Cornelius W. van Ranst filed ten different applications for patents covering the design of the powertrain, suspension, and running gear that were developed for the L-29 Cord. This is just one of the drawings, which illustrate four applications, filed between March and October 1929. On the earliest of the drawings, part number 7 is the change-speed transmission, located between engine and pinion gear. The splayed quarter-elliptic front springs would be used later by some race-car builders, including Myron Stevens. The length of the powertrain, from aft end of engine to the indispensable de Dion tube, was staggering, leaving the driving wheels with inadequate loading when accelerating or mounting inclines. *GBC ex ACD Museum*

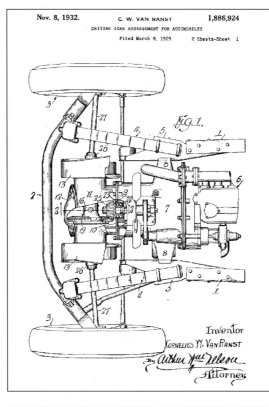

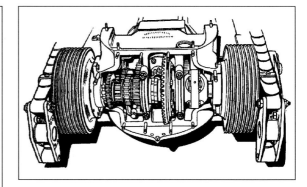

(above)

Miller Front-Drive, circa 1925

This artist's view of the interior of the Miller front-drive unit shows the arrangement and complexity of its parts. *GBC ex Peter Hull*

(below)

Miller 122 Front-Drive, 1925

The first Miller front-wheel-drive, instantly recognizable by its outboard brakes, which were soon replaced by inboard brakes. The car was sold to the Packard Motor Car Company at new retail price. Note the gunmetal grille and the front axle/de Dion tube.

GBC ex Packard Motor Car Co. Archives

Miller 122 Front-Drive, 1925
Many of the structural secrets of Miller front-wheel-drive were revealed in this photo of the second car brought from Indianapolis to France after the 1925 Indy race. *GBC ex Jackie Iuri/Guyot Collection*

Miller 122 Front-Drive, 1924
Cliff Durant feels out the second front-wheel-drive car at Culver City in November 1924. The car was still in its early prototype stage. Looking on were ace mechanic Harlan Fengler and famous race starter/steward Fred J. Wagner.
Joseph Freeman

61

(above)
Miller 91 Front-Drive, 1927
The Miller 91 engine of the Detroit Special was almost entirely hidden by its system of supercharging. Getting the plumbing to support the pressure was problematical. *IMS*

(above right)
Miller 122 Front-Drive, 1925
Miller's second front-wheel-drive was built for Cliff Durant, one of whose father's products was the new Locomobile Junior 8. Dave Evans was at the wheel, Riley Brett and Harry Miller standing alongside at the Altoona board speedway. *FU*

Miller 91 Front-Drive, 1926
Earl Cooper at Indy in 1926 in a photo inscribed by Miller to Albert Guyot, who was the agent in France for American Continental engines. Guyot also competed at Indy in 1926 but in an innovative car of his own creation, which broke a steering knuckle early in the race.
GBC ex Jackie Iuri/Guyot Collection

Miller 91 Front-Drive, 1927
Tommy Milton at the wheel of the 91 that he drove to eighth place in the 1927 Indy 500. The Detroit Special was financed and sometimes driven by Cliff Durant. Milton was its chief driver, and the car was engineered by him and Cornelius W. van Ranst. It pioneered two-stage supercharging and boasted 300 bhp; it was based upon Miller 91 front-wheel-drive components. At right is the turbine and supercharging expert of General Electric, Sanford G. Moss. *IMS*

Miller and Commercial Transmissions

During World War I young engineer Glover Ruckstell became a captain in the aviation branch of the US Army and was assigned to assist Colonel E. J. Hall with aero engine projects, including the famous Liberty engine. He of course worked at Hall-Scott, in Berkeley. He learned of the recently patented Perfecto two-speed planetary rear axle, the rights to which were held by the Perfecto Transmission & Differential Company of Seattle. Ruckstell thought of applying it to the Model T Ford, in order to give that two-speed car an additional two speeds. He obtained a license from Perfecto, established the Ruckstell Sales & Manufacturing Co. and arranged for the product to be fabricated by Hall-Scott. Henry Ford gave it his blessing and authorized its sale and installation by the Ford dealer network worldwide. Glover Ruckstell's

fortune was made. He dropped the Perfecto name and marketed his product as "The Ruckstell Axle—Four Speeds for Fords."

This enterprise was such a bonanza that Al Waddell went through the motions of quitting his job as advertising manager of Durant Motors of California in June 1921, in order to take over as sales manager for Ruckstell. A nation-wide organization was recruited from the ranks of the racing fraternity, starting with Eddie Pullen and Doc Caddy in Southern California. It was stated that Ruckstell and Miller had been close friends for many years. In September, Eddie Rickenbacker took over the states of Michigan and Ohio, while Tommy Milton spoke for Pennsylvania. Earl Cooper took Northern California. And so it went for the entire country, and it prospered.

In April 1922, Waddell returned to Durant,

Miller 91 Front-Drive, 1927
Marvelous photo of Ralph Hepburn clowning it up in the second front-wheel-drive car, which had been converted from a 122 to a 91. Standing by was Frank Elliott, who drove the car to tenth place at Indy that year. *GBC ex TW*

Miller 91 Front-Drive, 1928
Cliff Durant in the Detroit Special, which finished eighth at the Speedway in 1927. In 1928, Durant alternated at the wheel with Bob McDonough until the supercharger failed. *IMS*

Miller 91 Front-Drive, 1928
Starting lineup on the Altoona boards in August 1928, with Leon Duray in pole position and several front-drives just behind him. *Joseph Freeman*

as advertising manager. In October, National Champion, Murphy, joined the new Durant racing team, of which Harry Miller was the technical director. Goossen told me that he began laying out the Murphy front-wheel-drive in 1923; I failed to ask when. Murphy left the Durant team in March in order to concentrate upon his personal projects, presumably including the front-wheel-drive program. Toward the end of the year Ruckstell axle sales were approaching 100,000 units and sales were sure to double in 1924.

Into this situation stepped C. E. Starr, inventor of the Perfecto device and owner of the patent which covered it. He had invented a new accessory transmission which was said to be a big improvement over the one that already was a great success. The Starr Transmission Company was rushed into being, with a prominent Durant stockholder as president. Al Waddell was vice president in charge of sales and directors were Harry Miller and Jimmy Murphy. Miller and Starr went to the New York Auto Show together to present the new product to the industry. Together they returned to Los Angeles, where half the Miller plant was being converted to produce the new Starr transmission, while a second plant was being built in Oakland. Miller announced that he was ready to quit racing in order to commercialize various of his ideas. Murphy announced that he intended to do the same after the next Indy 500, and devote his full time to the transmission business.

C. E. Starr, who between 1917 and 1923 was granted US patents on nine different transmissions, divided his time between the Miller and the Oakland plants. His brother, Edgar, also a transmission expert, also worked at Miller's and helped him to produce the first few hundred transmissions.

These documented facts might relate in some way to how and why Miller, always a lover of simple, straightforward mechanical solutions, could suddenly reveal himself as a virtuoso of

Within the photograph: FRANK BRISCO, DRIVER. FLOYD WIESE, MECH. BRISCO ATKINSON SPECIAL. INDIANAPOLIS MOTOR SPEEDWAY, 1931.

Miller 91 Front-Drive, 1931
Old front-drive number one, always recognizable by its unique wheels and hubs, got a facelift and a 91 engine, and went on in the thick of battle for years out of mind. *IMS*

ultra-exotic transmission design.

With American top-level racing as its showcase, the Miller front-wheel-drive had a powerful impact both at home and abroad. Its limitations were not advertised and a corpus of folklore accumulated concerning its advantages. "It really was not good engineering," Leo admitted. "Let's say the final-drive ratio would be three to one. The way we did it, the torque was three times as great after it had left the pinion gear, because the ring gear turned only one-third as fast. The stresses on the change-speed mechanism and, in fact, on everything after the pinion, were magnified three times. The change-speed mechanism should be before the pinion, not after it. It did a fine job in oval-track racing but it never would do, in, say, a road machine."

The fact that Miller's patent was without commercial interest for industry did not mean that other solutions to the problem were not to be found. Among those who sensed that the time for a front-wheel-drive passenger car had come was Errett Lobban Cord, of Auburn, Cord, Duesenberg, AVCO, American Airlines and other manifestations of imagination and daring. Recognizing the value of Miller's name and cooperation, Cord put him on a retainer of $1000 per month for five years.

And he sent engineer Cornelius W. van Ranst— who had designed the good front-wheel-drive unit of Cliff Durant's Detroit Special—to the Miller plant to work with Leo Goossen on the creation of a system of front-wheel-drive which would use inexpensive standard components and would work on an ordinary road machine. "Leo did it," van Ranst told me. "He took those junk parts and did it. For me. I never could have done it by myself."

The general layout was that of a true Miller front-wheel-drive, although the transmission was oriented fore and aft, conventionally. It made the L-29 Cord car the supremely historic design which it forever will remain. It seemed to be an anomaly that none of that unique configuration had ever been applied for as a patent. Then, in 1979, I found a whole trove of information, spread over ten patents in the very rich archives of the Auburn-Cord-Duesenberg Museum in Auburn, Indiana. They all date from 1929 and all are in the name of C. W. van Ranst. All are assigned to Manning & Company, the financial core of the Cord empire. Miller's $60,000 income from Cord no doubt was intended to cover, at least in large part, this legal transfer of know-how, about which van Ranst did not speak and Goossen did not know. ■

Miller Four-Wheel-Drive, 1932

The sensation of the 1932 Indy 500 were two Miller four-wheel-drive entries. Gus Schrader's car was wrecked on lap seven when he smacked the wall. Bob McDonough, in this car's twin, went out ten laps later with engine damage caused by a broken oil line. In this photo, Bill White was standing behind the car's right rear tire. At the extreme right was Harry Miller's son, Ted, and next to him, wearing a cap, was Walt Sobraske. *IMS*

Chapter Nine: Miller Eights of the Thirties

Miller Factory, circa 1930
A concentration of some of the finest mechanical talent in the world. *GBC ex TW*

HARRY MILLER'S FORTUNES remained steadily ascendant throughout the Roaring Twenties. Then, just weeks before the crash of 1929, which would plunge the world into a decade of severe economic depression, he slipped into financially snug, worry-free retirement. His karma was radiant, and he had it made. This happened because E. L. Cord took a personal interest in him. In addition to paying Harry a nice monthly retainer, Cord recognized what a helpless innocent Miller was, in the business world, and began to worry about his welfare. Seeing the Crash coming, Cord kept urging Miller to bail out while he could. Miller didn't have any stock to unload, but he did have his business . . . and a standing offer from the Schofield interests to pay him $150,000 for it, in cash. That was a heap of money in 1929, and he finally followed Cord's urging, very shortly before the sky fell in. He was home free and, had he stayed there, his good karma might have lasted for the rest of his days.

He said "So long" to the wonderful old gang that had come that far with him, and embarked upon his retirement. To start with, he and Edna would become tourists, and see all of America from the luxurious comfort of one or another of Harry's three L-29 Cord cars. But at the age of 54, he was still a vigorous man, and marvelous ideas kept coming to him. Hanging out at the ranch and talking with the animals and his spirit friends didn't do it either. And so, in March of 1930, he set up a new engineering business, under the name of Rellimah, in a shop building on Venice near Alvarado, in Los Angeles. It soon became apparent that spelling his name backwards was pointless and the new company name became Harry A. Miller, Inc. He invested heavily in shop equipment and, with the decline of Miller-Schofield, he hired back most of his old staff. This initiative was far more ambitious than conditions justified.

While certain of Miller's concepts would be perpetuated by others in industry for decades to come, the master was eternally in pursuit of improved solutions to design problems. He had long since exhausted the possibilities of the wagon-sprung ladder-

Miller-Burden Roadster, 1930
William A. M. Burden was a New York financier, distinguished collector of modern art, and a lover of aviation and fine fast cars. He sponsored Miller's pioneering of four-wheel-drive and commissioned the construction of a four-wheel-drive, sixteen-cylinder sports car. Technically, it was one of the splendors of all time.
GBC ex William A. M. Burden

type frame. In order to arrive at a practical application of the front-drive principle, he created something new. Its base was a fairly wide and deep channel frame, with traditional kickups over the rear axle, but with the side-members chopped off short and abruptly at the front. In place of the classic "dumb irons," to which the front eyes of half-elliptic springs were pinned or shackled, there was this three-sided girder, the frame rail. To it was bolted a sturdy cast-bronze spring hanger to which were bolted, in turn, the butt ends of a pair of quarter-elliptic springs, one above the other. Their forward eyes encircled steel bolts which passed through ears which were integral parts of the de Dion tube's forged billet. The latter, of course, was the front axle in the Miller system of front-wheel-drive. Let it be repeated here that de Dion suspension has nothing to do with independent suspension. It is a means of making sprung weight out of what otherwise would be the dead weight of a heavy live axle, thus improving the adherence of tires to road.

Building on the success of the front-wheel-drive layout, Miller now welcomed a new decade of race-car engineering with a logical development of his front-wheel-drive theme. He applied exactly the same principle at the rear of his new rear-drive chassis, amputating the rear-axle kickups and installing trailing quarter-elliptics, in mirror image of the leading ones at the front. Inboard brakes were a nicety which he saved perhaps for a more prosperous moment. Along with the habitual

Hartford-type shock absorbers which he made himself, Miller added vane-type hydraulics, better to cushion the sharp jounce and rebound of his own severely stiff springs.

Unlike its highly specialized predecessors, the 1931 series Miller chassis was conceived as a sort of go-anywhere racing machine. It was intended to perform outstandingly, whether skimming over speedways or slogging around the dirt tracks which were totally replacing the boards.

The Miller Big Eights

For this basic workhorse Miller envisaged three power combinations. For economical racing on the dirt, a 200 ci, four-valve four. No one chose to order one of these. Then, he had a prototype 303 ci, 45 degree V-16 on hand, which still would fit under the car's deliberately broad and roomy hood. One such car was built for Bill White, but the engine itself proved disappointing.

Primarily for Indy, Miller imagined a large new pure-bred in-line eight. It was actually a return to his old love for the all-light-alloy, wet-steel-liner engine of the TNT and Golden Sub days. It retained the barrel crankcase which had rendered superb service, but it extended that casting all the way to the top of the cylinders. He used a pair of light-alloy heads, into which the liners were screwed; they used the inevitable rubber o-ring seals at their base. A bore and stroke of 3.125 x 3.75 in gave a 230 ci displacement which would become the designation of this series of engines, regardless of variations in bore and cubic capacity. Only two or three of the light-alloy engines were made and their o-rings leaked, as they did in his aero V-12 of 1917. Miller reacted with a direct return to the foolproof solution of two cast-iron blocks of four cylinders with integral heads. This solution prolonged the highly perfected straight-eight tradition of the twenties. These blocks were made with bores of 3.255 in and 3.375 in, giving displacements of 248.5 ci and 268.4 ci.

The so-called 230, or Big Eight, engines were distinguished by what have been called down-draft inlet ports, ever since their invention by Riley Brett in 1930. He employed them on Miller 91 cylinder blocks which he redesigned for the original Sampson Special U-16. Miller recognized the potential breathing and space-saving advantages of the design and, with Brett's accord, made it his own. As he had not done with previous straight-eights, Miller "siamesed" the inlet ports of the 230, meaning that a single external port served the internal ports of two adjacent cylinders. This compromise, which must have been difficult for Miller to accept, was imposed by space to accomodate only four single-throat carburetors on top of the engine. Super mechanic Cotton Henning considered it to be worth while to have blocks made which had an individual side port for each cylinder.

Miller headquarters had been transferred to their Gramercy Place location when the 1931-series production run was completed. It amounted to all of four chassis and a few extra engines.

Miller-Burden Special, 1930
Frontal view of the Burden bare chassis and Miller sixteen-cylinder engine.
GBC ex William A. M. Burden

One of course became the Bill White V-16, one was bought by Ralph Hepburn, and one single-seater, as well as a two-seater, went to car-owner Mike Boyle. One of the original aluminum-block engines was purchased by Louis Meyer, who installed it in a Myron Stevens-built car which then was running as a Jadson Special. These machines made their bow at Indianapolis that May, where Hepburn finished third in the 500, Meyer fourth, which was very good for new and untried equipment. The following year Bob Carey drove the Meyer car to a fourth-place finish at the Speedway and went on to win the AAA National Championship with that car. The next year, 1933, was a golden one for the big Eight, with Meyer driving the Hepburn car to a new speed record for the 500 miles of Indianapolis. These very competitive machines continued to lead good, active lives until the war. Two of them survive today.

The Miller Four-Wheel-Drive Cars

Although their great significance escaped most observers when Miller built these unique vehicles in 1931–1932, they were among the most important and prophetic ever to come from

Miller-Burden Special, 1930
Burden front-wheel brake and drive detail.
GBC ex William A. M. Burden

Miller Four-Wheel-Drive, 1932
Golden memories. Barney Oldfield visited the Miller plant to inspect the first of the four-wheel-drive machines to be completed. Although painted and apparently complete, the car seems not yet to have been under FWD Co. sponsorship. *IMS*

Miller Four-Wheel-Drive, 1932
The four-wheel-drive's chassis was another glorious piece of machinery. The 308 ci engine's two banks of cylinders formed an included angle of 45 degrees. Miller lost little time in adopting Riley Brett's downdraft ports. *IMS*

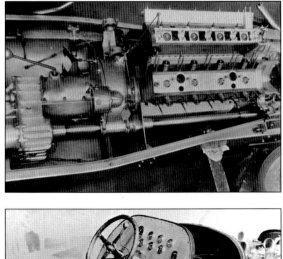

his fertile mind. Like their sisters of the 1931 series, they were extrapolated from the front-wheel-drives of the twenties. They differed radically in having the same De Dion drive system at both front and rear. Once one had mastered the art of transmitting engine torque through steered wheels, the ideal and multiple advantages of all-wheel drive were within one's grasp. The idea was not new, although it had not been used in a racing car since the first decade of the century, when Spyker and Christie were among the few who gave it a brief try. The idea probably came to Miller early in his front-wheel-drive period, but it was not until the fall of 1931 that he explained to draftsmen Goossen and Everett Stevenson what he wanted, and for all of the good reasons that we know today.

The general layout was perfectly simple. The engine was mounted conventionally at the front of the chassis. Behind it were a clutch and three-speed transmission, and then an amidships box of transfer gears which extended toward the right-hand frame rail. From that offset position, driveshafts extended fore and aft to final-drive units

4 wheel drive
(Front)

Miller Four-Wheel-Drive, 1932
To minimize width, the angle between the
banks of cylinders was only 45 degrees.
Valve-included angle was 80 degrees. Here
one has a perfect view of the first split
crankcase on a Miller racing engine. The
front transfer case for the four-wheel-drive
layout was similar to earlier Miller front-
wheel-drives, but this car's four-wheel-
drive unit included a reservoir for engine
oil. *IMS*

from which the front and rear half-axles emerged. Each unit contained a differential, as did the transfer case, compensating for all inequalities in rates of rotation. With it, one could hope to transmit twice the tractive effort possible with two-wheel-drive before wheelspin set in. It had other virtues for road vehicles. It could be a fantastic breakthrough, if it would work.

Those who knew him said that Harry Miller was a man who would gamble his last dollar on the drawing board. This seemed to be a sure-shot occasion, one in which he held all the trump cards. We have only faint glimmerings of what actually happened. It was probably his well-placed patron, E. L. Cord, who put him in touch with Wall Street financiers Victor Emmanuel and William A. M. Burden. Both had considerable wealth and both loved fine, fast cars. Both were cosmopolitan—Burden became US Ambassador to Belgium, although he wanted France. Both liked road racing, European style, and wanted to see American racing cars on European starting grids. They were men who could find the means to do big things.

Miller went to New York to confer with these gentlemen, taking Goossen along, as an articulate and literate four man. Miller was speechless in their palatial towers and grumbled that "they talk engines like fools." But that was all right. He had pitched each of them a sports car to end them all. It would have sixteen cylinders, four overhead camshafts, and a big Roots blower. And to get those barrels of horsepower to the pavement, they would have Miller's new breakthrough—front wheel drive. Price, $35,000 a copy.

This much can be verified in Burden's 1982 autobiography, *Peggy and I*, along with the fact that Emmanuel "had gotten tired of doling out money and seeing no car and had cancelled his order."

It was at this point, I believe, that Miller sought and obtained sponsorship for one of his new racing cars by the FWD Co., which then manufactured trucks and fire engines in Clintonville, Wisconsin. In other words, under

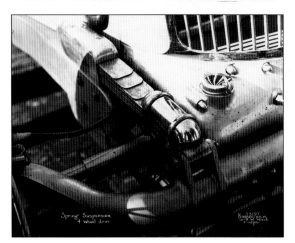

(*above*)
Miller Four-Wheel-Drive, 1932
While the board of directors of the Four-Wheel-Drive Auto Company went to Indianapolis by train, employee Bill Smith drove the firm's old scout car, Nancy Hanks, from Clintonville, Wisconsin, to mark the occasion. *IMS*

(*left*)
Miller Four-Wheel-Drive, 1932
The original transfer case, behind the change-speed transmission, from which shafts ran fore and aft to their respective transaxles. The FWD Co. insisted upon a more sophisticated design, incorporating its own differential. *IMS*

Miller Four-Wheel-Drive, 1932
The brakes were cable-operated and the absence of shock absorbers was startling. The shiny U-bolted object in which the photographer was reflected was an adjustable spring-clamp pad. In original Miller front-drives, the front-drive unit also served as the bottom header tank of the car's radiator; that may also have been the case with the four-wheel-drives. *IMS*

Miller Eight, 1933
Lou Meyer drove the Miller eight-cylinder 258 ci Tydol Special to win the 1933 Indy 500. *IMS*

the original arrangement each of the sports cars may have been part of a package deal which was based upon race-car sponsorship. Thus, Emmanuel vanished from the scene, while Burden hung on. Burden was officially listed as the entrant of one of the race cars, and eventually took or seized possession of a one-off flight of mechanical fantasy with all of its teething troubles impeccably intact.

These race cars, powered by a 45 degree four-camshaft v-8, were imagined by Miller and engineered by Goossen. Bore and stroke were a neat 3.50 x 4.00 in and displacement was 308 ci. Output might have been as high as 350 bhp. The cylinder block/head castings were of iron, each incorporating a pair of siamesed down-draft inlet ports. The crankshaft was of the 180 degree, single-plane type. What was notable above all about the engine was its crankcase which, rather than being of the barrel type which had served Miller so long and well, was split conventionally, just a bit below the crankshaft center line. We have

74

here the beginning of the new family of engines which would lead to the Aero 255 the following year, the Gulfs and, finally, the rest of those that were built or projected by Miller to the end of his career.

Racing the Four-Wheel-Drives

At Indy in 1932 the two four-wheel-drives performed very well in practice and attained good qualifying speeds in the hands of Gus Schrader in the Burden car and Bob McDonough in the FWD. But Miller's luck had abandoned him. From the fall of the starting flag Schrader showed absolutely brilliant speed and maneuverability. But, on merely the seventh lap, oil from his engine got on a tire as he was charging through a turn, the tire broke loose, and he lost control and crashed, happily with little damage to car or occupants. McDonough did little better, being forced to drop out on lap 17 due, it was said, to something as banal as a broken oil line. Thus the revolutionary new cars had no opportunity to demonstrate what they could do, and Miller was left to his rendezvous with financial ruin.

In 1933, Frank Brisko practically flew in the FWD Co. car to a new Indy qualifying average speed of 118.388 mph—second fastest in a starting field of forty-two cars, and just a tenth of an mph slower than the fastest of them all. But this time it was overheated oil that put the car out of the race on lap 37, and the failure image of four-wheel-drive became more deeply etched in the mass mentality.

The following year, 1934, Pete De Paolo was invited to drive in the Grand Prix of Tripoli, on what was probably the world's fastest road circuit. The retired De Paolo found himself a ride in the ex-Schrader (Burden) car, which car-owner Frank Scully had picked up from Miller for $1,600. With it, Pete went the full 326-mile distance on the North African circuit, racing against a field of Alfas, Maseratis, and a single Bugatti. He finished seventh, 12 minutes behind Varzi's winning P3 Alfa Romeo. Rather significantly, he was a mere 12 seconds slower for the distance than René Dreyfus' Type 59 Bugatti, a pretty good road-racing machine, prepared by its factory. Following that eminently respectable exploit, De Paolo took the start in the also-superfast AVUS GP at Berlin, where he was lying third when a connecting rod let go. The performance of the car on this junket lends credence to the idea that the four-wheel-drives were conceived with road as well as track racing in mind.

The main point is that Miller invented modern four-wheel-drive, just as surely as he invented modern front-wheel-drive. Had the chips fallen differently, the four-wheel-drive revolution would have begun in 1932, instead of several decades later. Both of the wonderfully historic original cars happily are preserved today. ∎

Miller V-16, 1931
On the eve of leaving for the Speedway, Miller and his collaborators pose with the new V-16 303 ci car. From left, Bill White, Cantlon, Miller, Doc Caddy. The car's suspension was symmetrical: de Dion axles and quarter-elliptic springs at both ends. *GBC ex TW*

Miller-Ford, 1935
The cars were the state of the art at the
time. Even the suspension members
themselves are streamlined. *GBC ex FMC*

Chapter Ten: The Miller-Fords

Miller 151 Marine, circa 1928
B116 Angeles I was a lovely example of a little racing hydroplane proudly adorned with a gleaming, unblown Miller 151.
GBC ex Dick Loynes

I T APPEARS TO HAVE BEEN while Miller was holding forth on Venice Boulevard that a new personage entered his life. He was a salesman of cars and other merchandise named Preston Tucker. The Rosen Papers contain a letter on the stationery of Harry A. Miller, Inc., dated December 16, 1931. It is addressed to the Assistant Secretary of the Navy and goes on for two single-spaced pages in this vein:

"Dear Sir: Would like to have your advice on ways and means of obtaining an order from the Government to build some large aeronautical motors, power ranging from 1000, 2000, and 3000 horsepower motors." It closes with "Very truly yours, Preston Tucker, Sales Manager." Mark Dees cites similar correspondence addressed to top brass of the US Air Corps.

Nothing came from these initiatives of Tucker, who was domiciled in Detroit. The real sales manager of the company was Harry's son Ted who, at Venice Boulevard and then at Gramercy Place, tried to find buyers for four-cylinder racing engines at $2,000 a copy. On the very rare occasions when one would materialize there was joy in the plant, and some back wages could be paid. Finally, on July 8, 1933, the inevitable moment of reckoning arrived: outside creditors filed suit and Miller was placed in involuntary bankruptcy. He was wiped out—out of business, home, ranch, animals, and a big spread that he had acquired near beautiful Jackson Hole, Wyoming. His world was smashed, but so were the worlds of loyal friends who had stood by him through thick and thin and who had made it possible for him to become supreme in his domain. Crushed by humiliation and guilt, Miller turned his back on the region and culture that he had helped to build and, that December, migrated east, with Edna and Ted.

Ted recalled that "Tucker had somehow arranged for my father to build fifty armored cars for what was then the Persian government, and to do it in the Marmon plant in Indianapolis." It was to be a joint Miller-Tucker venture, and Harry insisted upon the constitution of a proper corporate entity to insure the legal character of the enterprise. Local functionaries stalled until he finally flew to Delaware and created a correct legal framework for the operation. It took until mid-February 1934 to arrive at this point, when the financial backer of this operation committed suicide, and the plan fell to pieces.

Ted drove his parents to Michigan in an L-29 Cord, where they spent the rest of the winter with friends. Both Ted and Tucker spent that summer working for a large Detroit brewery. Ted drove a beer truck and, in his free time, helped Tucker collect proxies to serve in a takeover effort aimed at their employer. Tucker miscalculated the number of proxies that he would have to have, and he and his accomplice were released from the firm. On the heels of that event there came, in Ted's memory, the begin-

ning of the Miller-Ford spectacle. It is at this point that the Miller scenario starts becoming somewhat hallucinatory.

The Junk Formula

The basic idea was absolutely the soundest in the world. Machinery purists looked down on "the Junk Formula," however this new displacement allowance (1) made it cost less to go racing and (2) stimulate industry participation therein. Starting in 1930 the maximum limit on displacement shot from 91.5 to a staggering 366 ci. Superchargers were banned unless you were driving a two-stroke, and so were more than two valves per cylinder.

Miller 151 Marine, 1926
Harlan Fengler with an early marine 155.
FU

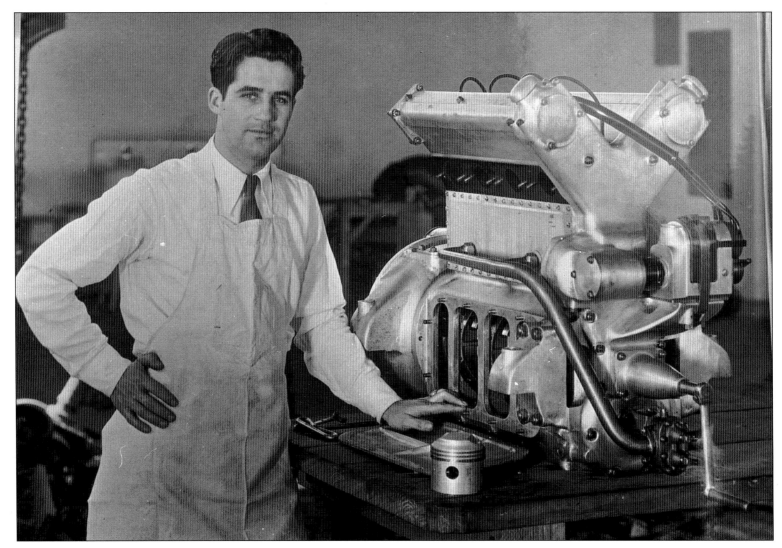

Carburetion became a shadow of its old self and fuel consumption became restricted. No car could weigh less than 1750 lb, or less than 7.5 lb per ci. And so on. In spite of thus being bound and gagged, the top winners continued to be thoroughbreds of relatively modest displacement. However, engineers and mechanics working with stock-blocks became increasingly adept, and already by 1932, a 366 ci mass of South Bend iron, entered by the Studebaker factory, was herded by Cliff Bergere into a most impressive third place in the Indy 500. Thus encouraged, Studebaker went all-out for 1933 and prepared a team of five quite splendid cars. In the Indianapolis race they simply ran like trains from start to finish, placing seventh, ninth, tenth, eleventh and twelfth. Private Studebaker entries finished sixth and eighth, making for a cavalcade, the publicity fallout of which made the whole exercise highly rewarding. Beyond that, a Buick-powered car finished well up in the money, in fifth place. The top four places went to Millers. The following year, 1934, there were only three, instead of six, stock-block cars in the top ten, but there was a good sprinkling of them elsewhere throughout the field, including a couple of Ford v-8s. They excited interest but did little, except for one which made an exit over the south-west wall on lap 33.

With both Miller and Tucker in Michigan, and substantially at liberty, they turned their attention to the stock-block phenomenon at some time in the last half of 1934. Any good sponsor would do, but Ford was the perfect partner. The company had released its trusty v-8 just two years before. It was by far the hottest performing engine in the low-price field, and the company was already working actively on the development of a performance image and had been dabbling in road racing. The logical ultimate goal would be Indianapolis and the whole Championship Trail. But what could one hope to win and to prove? That one was the stock-block best? Or might one be able to be the best, period? After all, Bergere's Studebaker in 1932 came within two places of doing it. Certainly the combined resources of Harry Miller and the going Ford v-8 engine could make up the difference. One can imagine arch-enthusiast Tucker leaping to accept such an argument. For a man with Miller's knowledge of the realities at stake, it is almost unimaginable.

Miller Four, 1930
A gorgeous Bill White four, driven by Bugs Allen. *GBC*

Miller-Ford, 1935
The front-wheel-drive Miller-Fords were absolutely brilliant in design, conception, and execution, but the project was launched so late that they never had a chance. *GBC ex FMC*

Miller-Ford, 1935

A bare chassis and a feast for the eyes. The V-8 engines were equipped with four carburetors. What appeared to be axle fairings extending from the front-drive unit were in fact streamlined suspension control arms. *GBC ex FMC*

Even if you do succeed in making a silk purse out of a sow's ear, it will never match the real thing.

Let us pause to say parenthetically that there is a very nice body of literature on the Miller-Ford adventure. First, and in chronological order, there is a very penetrating, staff-written technical report in *Automotive Industries* for June 1, 1935. It was researched before there were any complete cars to photograph. Then there is a choice retrospective piece in *Car Life* for June 1965, by J. L. Heisler. Additionally there is a chapter in Leo Levine's 1968 book, *Ford: The Dust And The Glory*, for which the author had access to important company sources. Lastly there is Mark Dees' analysis of the subject in his *The Miller Dynasty*. Each deals with the theme in a different but always enriching manner.

Preston Tucker and the Miller-Ford Deal

Levine states that the idea to build a huge team of Ford-powered cars under Ford patronage originated with Tucker at some unspecified time after the 1934 Indy race. He says that the idea

appealed to Miller, who began to develop design ideas and to seek out good drivers to man the machines, when they should exist. It was Tucker's job, of course, to promote the idea. He had worked for Ford at one time and was able to present the general idea to Henry Ford's son, Edsel. Edsel then took the ball and tried to sell the idea within the company, the hardest sell of which was to his father. He succeeded in obtaining old Henry's approval, after which the problem became that of inserting the program into the vital processes of the giant corporation. Up to this point we have no dates whatsoever, but there would seem to have been adequate time for the construction of ten identical racing cars, using many in-house mechanical parts, notably engines.

The buck, however, was passed from one person or department to another, without the project finding a home. Our first firm date is January 21, 1935, when Tucker submitted a written cost specification for the project to Ford's assistant general sales manager. Tucker wrote, "We agree to complete the ten cars by May 10th, 1935, and will then enter them in the Indianapolis 500-mile race." This means that there remained, as of that moment, 111 days in which to conjure up ten very sophisticated but nonexistent machines.

The cost to Ford for this service would be $25,000. The amount is so jarringly unreal that it should trigger a second set of alarms, backing up the first offense to the reader's credulity. And then Mr. Tucker closed with, "It is our sincere belief that these cars will finish 1-2-3." He didn't even have a draftsman yet, but was predicting—sincerely—an outcome of a race which would contradict all past experience. Again, no alarms seemed to go off. Tucker also failed to stipulate that title to the whole fleet of cars would remain snugly with Miller-Tucker, Inc. Would you buy a used car from this man? Henry Ford would even buy ten.

A prudent prospective sponsor would have been likely to reject the plan at this point. Instead, Ford accepted the deal, while tossing it to N. W. Ayer, its advertising agency at the time, on February 7. "Then, later in the month, Ayer and Miller-Tucker got together on paper." This would seem to indicate that they signed a contract. The getting-together committed someone to pay an unexplained, supplementary $50,000 to Miller-Tucker. At that point Miller could feel safe in bidding a crack draftsman, Everett Stevenson, to come to Detroit from California, to get to work on the drawings. Stevenson thought that he was being summoned merely for a couple of days' consultation, not to be plunged into a maelstrom.

Levine elucidates that "The machines, equipment, etc., that Tucker borrowed from Ford for their workshop in Detroit [where the cars were to be built] didn't arrive until March 12." Using the original deadline of May 10, that left exactly sixty days for outfitting the shop with machine tools and so on, completing the design and working drawings of the car, building the ten avant-garde vehi-

Miller-Ford, 1935
The desperate search for enough
horsepower to qualify. Here, the V-8 had
just two carburetors, and even without the
one ram-tuning stack that has been
installed they seem to be higher than the
line of the engine hood. *GBC ex Autolite*

Miller-Ford, 1935
The assembly shop in Detroit where the beautiful cars were built to an impossible time limit. Note the moment of truth chalked on three columns: May 30—the day before the race. *GBC ex Autolite*

cles, and testing and developing them—the indispensable sorting-out process. This was patently ridiculous and was equivalent to a deliberate planning of disaster. All commentators, including Leo Levine, are unanimously in agreement that there simply was not the time in which to do what absolutely had to be done.

The project was not going to cost the Ford Motor Company anything. The cost of Miller-Tucker services would be prorated among the members of Ford's vast dealer network. Thus, as Levine points out, each dealer owned a piece of the cars to be, or of one of them. They became passionately engaged in the project, pulling for that sweeping victory and its effect upon their Depression-strangled sales.

The inevitable happened. The cars were rushed together in an environment of unrelieved panic, twenty-four hours a day and seven days a week. Only four cars ever qualified for the race. They all retired, and all for the same reason: a blocked steering gearbox which an absolute modicum of run-in time would have demonstrated to be defective. It could have been rendered perfectly operational if the merest minutes of practice time had been available.

But we are concerned with machinery only indirectly in this chapter. Its really important content is the second venting of the wrath of the gods against Harry Miller. The moral and material scars of his devastating bankruptcy were still fresh, and now what had he done? Used as a pawn, he had been placed in an impossible position, on the world stage front-center. Once more, he had crashed and burned in humiliating defeat. And whom had he carried with him, or seemed to have betrayed? Well, the Ford dealer body, individually and as a group. All of the wonderful guys, the wonderfully gifted artists in metal who were the absolute salt of the earth to him, who had fought on the barricades at his side to…to make some hustler's dream live. And then there was the unimaginably vast Ford Motor Company, which had been the biggest victim of this fiasco. And, finally, there was Mr. Henry Ford, himself. He was a hero-figure to half the

world, and he had been reduced to ridicule because he, like so many others, had had confidence in the worth of Harry A. Miller. During the final two or three weeks Mr. Ford, Edsel, and the justly feared Harry Bennett had come to the shop daily, to witness the poor progress that each day brought, and to grind their teeth and to curse.

I have the feeling that Harry Miller never was held responsible for what had happened, for this blatant folly. I believe that the only reason for which the arch-pragmatic Ford organization held still for it was that Mr. Ford, personally, liked it. That it was he who went along with Tucker's fantasies of one-two-three stock-block victories, and who decreed, "Let it be." And I like to think that he may have said to Miller, "You know my fondness for planetary gears. Well, I have an idea for a new steering setup, and I want you to use it in our cars." And that is why there were no recriminations from Ford against Miller in the aftermath. And that is why, Harry Bennett invited Ted Miller to name the Ford plant where he'd like to have a good job, anywhere in the world.

The Miller-Ford Cars

As for the cars, to begin with and in spite of their having been born out of chaos, they had terrific class. Class in bodywork and class in mechanical design and execution. A metal artist named Ernie Weil was in charge of the latter. Next, they were utterly beautiful, among the most flawless of the entire oval-track breed of vehicles. Another great artist, Emil Diedt, shaped the body panels. The cars were extremely low, abetted by front-wheel-drive with its elimination of the conventional driveshaft. Levine sees in them anticipation of the Indy "roadsters" of the fifties. Their front-wheel-drive unit had two forward speeds and a reverse gear, still on the wrong side of the pinion, but one hears that it worked pretty well. The suspension was independent, front and rear, by means of double transverse leaf springs and upper and lower control arms of slightly unequal length. These "arms" were more like rectangular plates which were sculptured to form a sort of airfoil enclosure for half-shaft and springs, when in place. The entire car was of that sort of immaculate design that inspires use of the adjective "sanitary."

None of the sources is of help in sorting out the provenance of various assemblies, although all do say that different elements came from different Ford shops; some at Highland Park, some from the River Rouge plant, and so on. The engines, for example, were built up elsewhere, and not all in one shop. The horsepower output that has come down to us is 150 at 5000 rpm, but that is just a ballpark figure. When, just days before the race, it was found how slow the cars were, various experiments were made, such as a variety of different carburetion arrangements. Levine tells how souped-up engines were ripped out of racing speedboats on the Canadian side of the Detroit River and rushed to the Speedway. So that whole sector, that of power, was outside of Miller's jurisdiction.

After the race and the fiasco, and disregarding Miller-Tucker's contractual title to the cars, Henry Ford himself ordered seizure of them all. He had them hauled away, to be gotten out of sight for a couple of years or so. Enraged though he was, he appreciated what was fine in the cars sufficiently so as not to destroy them, but to preserve them and release them into private hands as time went by. Thus, all ten still exist today.

The Miller-Ford episode dealt a devastating but passing blow to the Ford image. Harry Miller was the fall guy for the unrealizable fantasies of others, in which he allowed himself to become enmeshed. ■

Miller-Ford, 1935
A seemingly dejected driver ignores the camera. Four cars mustered enough speed to qualify for the starting grid. All fell victims to a steering-gear defect that a few hours' development time would have revealed in advance. In 1946, one of the Miller-Fords was resurrected to set the fastest lap ever at Indy by a side-valve engine: 118.890 mph. *GBC ex Autolite*

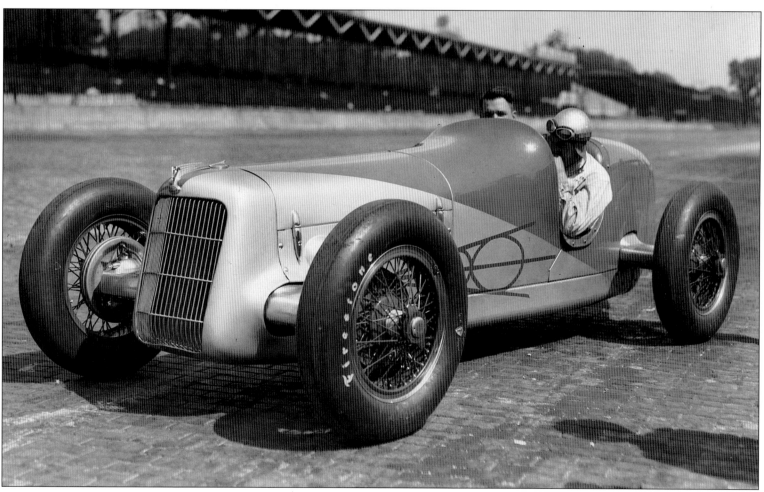

Miller-Gulf Four, 1938
The first four-cylinder front-engined Miller-Gulfs wore their radiator tubing on the nose, presenting an avant garde streamlined visage. The Gulf cars used Miller-Ford-type suspension as well as disc brakes, which at least were beautifully ornamental. *SM*

Chapter Eleven: The Miller-Gulfs

Miller Four, 1934

While Fred Offenhauser and his successors would remain staunchly loyal to traditional Miller design, the old master himself blazed new trails. His first new design, a 255 ci four, was a return to the technique that he had used with his single-cam fours of the Golden Submarine type.

GBC ex Lou Bromme

HERE IS THE STORY of these cars, what they were like, and what became of them. Even more basic is the story of why they existed at all, and what they were expected to accomplish. In 1953, when primary witnesses were still there, I wrote to a top executive of Gulf Research & Development, asking:

"How was the Gulf car project conceived, and by whom? When did it begin and end? How much was spent on it?"

The prompt response to those specific questions was:

"The primary purpose of the Gulf racing car program was to demonstrate the quality of our automotive products. The cost of this project is confidential."

The most casual observer of this fabulous and incredibly ill-fated program could tell that its cost had been a secondary consideration at best. But how did the sponsors expect to demonstrate the quality of their products by committing themselves to the use of their 81-octane No Nox pump gasoline in competition against a howling herd of machines that were exquisitely set up to derive all of the benefits inherent in methanol fuel, laced with secret substances? My God, the Miller-Gulf of 1938 developed 83 bhp/liter at best, while the contemporary Sparks-Thorne six pulled 132. You could demonstrate how to use No Nox and finish dead last.

The Beginnings of the Miller-Gulf Cars

How did it all start? Speaking of the Miller-Ford aftermath and the summer of 1935, Ted Miller told me, "My father was going regularly to Pittsburgh, to talk with Colonel Drake of the Gulf Oil Company. They got to be quite good pals. They got together [in a business way] a year or two after that."

Mark Dees retraces the story thus: After the bankruptcy in 1933 and before eviction from his home on Chevy Chase Drive in Los Angeles, Miller conceived a lightweight twin-cam four, obviously for aircraft use since it had dual ignition, by a pair of magnetos. It had the same bore and stroke as the existing iron-block Miller 255, but it used light alloy as extensively as possible, along with steel wet liners, two valves per

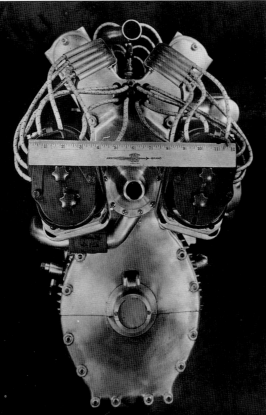

(*above*)
Miller Four, 1934
Dual magnetos and twin updraft carburetors of the new Miller 255 ci four.
GBC ex Lou Bromme

(*right*)
Miller Four, 1934
Straight on view of the four showing the amazingly narrow width of the engine.
GBC ex Lou Bromme

cylinder, detachable head and conventional split crankcase. All this was drawn up by Everett Stevenson but, due to the priority of other events, the project progressed no further at that time. Then, in early 1937, Miller's first client for a straight-eight engine, Ira Vail, reappeared in his life. No longer a driver but still a racing entrepreneur, Vail commissioned the design and construction of a pair of new machines to compete against the technology which then reigned on the dirt tracks and at Indianapolis. Miller had the answer to the engine requirement in his already designed aluminum 255 which, with a 0.125 in overbore, could be made into a 270.

The chassis which he proposed was very imaginative, certainly in terms of American practice, which still harked back to pre-World War I technique. It had deep, rolled-steel side members which were intended to be ultra-stiff. Then all-round independent suspension was a refinement of the Miller-Ford type. The engine and clutch were at the front of the vehicle, the transmission and final drive at the rear, meaning that the driveshaft always turned at crankshaft speed.

The brakes were truly another Miller first. They utilized discs, but are not to be confused with or considered to be anticipations of the now-classic disc brake of the caliper type. They were based upon an entirely different principle, that of the disc clutch and its pressure plate. As designed and executed by Miller, they looked wonderful. As for their effectiveness, no one ever made further application of the idea. Another spectacular, seeming breakthrough was Miller's replacement of the conventional radiator core with a highly decorative sort of trellis of rather large-bore chromed tubing which was wrapped around the car's hood, throughout its full length. A final great innovation was the employment of external fuel tanks, one on each side of the car, and at the level of the frame. They were interconnected, so that weight distribution would be in equilibrium regardless of the quantity of fuel aboard.

The story goes that the construction of these two cars was just getting nicely under way when the son of Gulf's board chairman, James F. Drake, Jr., dropped in at Miller's shop, and the rest is history. Ira Vail was bought out and the entire project was moved to the headquarters of the Gulf R&D Company at Harmarville, a suburb of Pittsburgh. As work continued on the fours, a program was launched immediately for the design and construction of a team of much more ambitious four-wheel-drive, rear-engine Gulf sixes. They, too, would run exclusively on 81 octane Gulf No Nox gas.

There had been a revolution in the racing regulations for Indianapolis. The 366 ci formula, which barred superchargers, had been in force from 1930 until after the 1936 race. Then it was announced that, for the coming year, supercharging would be allowed, while displacement would remain unchanged. Also new was the provision that all entries must run on pump gasoline. Thus supercharging re-entered American Championship racing with 11 blown engines at Indy in

Miller-Gulf Four, 1938
Front-engined Gulf four with the intermediate-type external radiator core. This radiator development also proved to be inadequate. The cars stood extremely high. *SM*

1937, in spite of which advantage the 500 was won by a thumping, unblown Offy 255. And Harry Miller, the generally recognized master of automotive supercharging in the United States, naturally took advantage of the new rules to include a very impressive blower in the specification of the avant-garde new car that he was laying out for Gulf. The

Miller-Gulf Six, 1941
The bare chassis of the Gulf six. While its general layout was inspired by the German Auto Unions of the 1930s, it was radically original in most details, large and small. Its chassis side-members doubled as fuel tanks for the pump gasoline that it burned. *GBC ex GRDC*

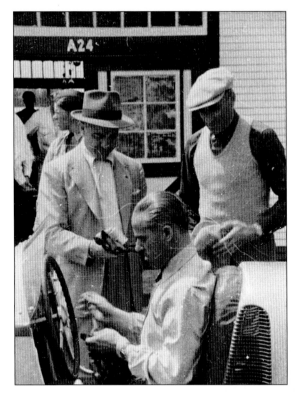

Miller-Gulf, 1938
In 1938, rumours flew that Gulf would race in European Grands Prix. Here, in the garage at Indy, the great Italian champion Tazio Nuvolari inspected one of the Millers as Peter De Paolo, wearing hat, looked on.
SM

(*above right*)
Miller-Gulf Six, 1938
Harry Miller himself gunning the throttle during tuning operations before that year's ill-fated Indy 500. In 1938, the supercharger was of the Roots type, as one can see here. *SM*

(*right*)
Miller Six, 1939
The powerhouse that howled Miller's swan song: rear view of his Gulf six with its centrifugal supercharger in the foreground. For it, Miller went back to designing his own special carburetors. Note the 45-degree inclination of the cylinder block.
GBC ex GRDC

recent highly international Vanderbilt Cup races had had a huge effect upon public interest at home and abroad, which encouraged Gulf to include participation in European Grands Prix among its goals. Hence the blower chosen by Miller was of the Roots type, by far the best for the broad-range rpm requirements of road racing.

He also chose six cylinders in line, a configuration with which he had almost zero experience. If an in-line eight would have made his power train too long, why not a v-8, about which he possessed at least a certain amount of personal expertise? That question remains enigmatic, whereas his reason for choosing only 180.4 ci, rather than the full 366 that were allowed in 1937 is clear enough. After that year's Indy race, Speedway president Eddie Rickenbacker announced that, for the next two years, the track was getting precisely in line with the international trend. The new Indy regulations would be those of the AIACR—the pre-World War II forerunner of the FIA and FISA—for Grand Prix racing: three liter, 183 ci blown and 4.5 liters, 274 ci unblown. There would be no restrictions whatsoever on fuel. This meant that Gulf would be up against methanol and worse, which for some reason was not a deterrent. Seeking a logical explanation for this decision to go into battle with inferior weapons, I wrote in *Sports Cars Illustrated* for May 1958:

"Gulf was ready to go racing, if the machine

Miller-Gulf Six, 1939

Driver George Barringer contemplates the immensely long inline six-cylinder power package. Integral with it is the rear transaxle gear housing, and behind that, the supercharger. *GBC ex GRDC*

Miller-Gulf Six, 1939

Top view of the engine, minus camshaft housings and valve cups. Curiously, the spark-plug bosses and even their cups were not concentric with and parallel to the cylinder axes, but were inclined toward the front of the engine. *GBC ex GRDC*

Miller-Gulf Six, 1939

Looking up into the cylinder bores, one sees that the spark plugs were indeed off-center and inclined. This perhaps was a tradeoff in order to gain slightly increased valve diameter. There were seven main bearings. *GBC ex GRDC*

Miller-Gulf Six, 1941
The Gulf six's independent rear suspension was based upon the upper and lower transverse-spring system that Miller had first used on the Miller-Fords of 1935.
GBC ex GRDC

were available that could perform excellently, using the company's then 80-octane No Nox gasoline and Gulfpride oil. Miller convinced his new patron that he had the package that could do just that."

I submitted this hypothesis to Gulf R&D for screening and it came back with the statement, "Thank you. There is nothing here that we object to."

The cars were so high and slab-sided that it was hard to imagine them having come from the same hand and brain as those which had created the Miller-Fords. While the objective seemed to be the same, the ways of getting there were worlds apart. At the Speedway in '38 those bizarre, quasi-aircraft-type cooling systems shook themselves apart and were replaced in a very improvised-looking way by ordinary rectangular radiator cores which were mounted longitudinally on either side of the engine hood. This did not remedy the cooling problem and neither car managed to qualify for the race, bringing back ugly and painful memories of 1935. Taken back to Harmarville, the cars were fitted with the usual internal radiator cores and eventually disposed of to Miller's associate, Preston Tucker.

Developing the Miller-Gulf Sixes

The first Gulf six had very much the upright-piano form of the fours. Chassis-wise and from a technical standpoint it was dazzlingly, excitingly different from everything in the world, although it did share rear-central engine location with Germany's Auto Union. The engine, which obviously belonged to the same design family as the aero four, was the world's first to have oversquare bore/stroke dimensions—barring some antediluvian ancestor. The dimensions were 3.50 x 3.125 in. All light-alloy construction again was used, block integral with a split crankcase, and cylinders inclined at a built-in 45 degrees to the case. The big, three-lobe Roots blower was driven directly off the aft end of the seven main-bearing crankshaft. The inlet ports were siamesed in the detachable head and an experimental "extractor" exhaust system was tried—another Miller first.

Again the engine was offset in the frame. Power flow was from it to a front-mounted four-speed transmission, from which it was transmitted in two directions: (1) forward to a front differential and (2) back to a rear differential. The massive transmission included the front-axle differential and the transfer gears for the driveshaft which drove the front and rear axles. Three final-drive ratios were made available by meshing any one of three transfer gears on the front-and-rear-axle driveshaft with the transmission cluster gears. It sounds complicated, and was. The shafting which passed under the driver's seat forced the seat to be a foot and a half above the ground—again, a high seating position. To shelter the driver, then, the body had to be higher than the chassis itself required. Miller used side fuel tanks again and, continuing his experiments with engine cooling, he tried a new type of surface radiator on each side of the little cabin which occupied the usual place of an engine hood. There was a distinct aircraft feel to the vehicle as a whole, which may have been a clue to Miller's longer-range interests. The car was rushed to a semblance of completion in time to command the rather fascinated attention of the automotive world on the occasion of the Indy 500 in 1938. For simple lack of power, among myriad teething troubles, it was unable to qualify for the race. So, back to Harmarville, and the drawing board.

The car was radically redesigned. The Roots blower was replaced by another Miller innovation, a centrifugal supercharger with an impeller which had, for the first time, working surfaces on both sides, instead of only one. It delivered its more or less doubled charge to a beautiful new light-alloy intercooler. New patterns, castings, and cylinder heads with individual inlet ports were made. The extractor exhaust system gave way to long, curved, individual vertical pipes. A conventional radiator core was adopted, and numerous body changes were made. At bewildering cost, three new cars were completed and entered for the Indy 500 of 1939.

In pre-qualifying practice driver Johnny Seymour lost control of his Gulf car and hit the wall. One of its side-mounted fuel tanks ruptured and the car exploded into flame and was totally destroyed, Seymour managing to escape with slight injuries. This may have had a sobering effect on teammate Zeke Meyer, who decided that he didn't trust the car's handling and withdrew from the team. He was not replaced. The third Gulf driver, George Bailey, qualified his machine into a respectable sixth place on the grid, but lasted only forty-seven laps before his engine dropped a valve.

In 1940, three cars, in tip-top shape, were sent to the Speedway. This time it was Bailey who crashed in practice. Again a side tank ruptured and the car went up in flames, taking the driver's life with it. Officials "suggested" that the two surviving cars be withdrawn, and they were.

Were these crashes due to treacherous handling, as Zeke Meyer felt? Gulf decided to settle the question and a few weeks later sent a car and crew to one of the world's safest racing courses, the Bonneville Salt Flats, for thorough testing of its handling at high speeds. George Barringer was entrusted with the driving and he left no trace of doubt that the car's handling was above reproach. With this reassuring knowledge, and being on Ab Jenkins' surveyed site, it was arranged to make an attack on the existing AIACR International Class D records, up to 500 miles. On July 30, 1940 Barringer broke every one by a wide margin, from

Miller-Gulf Six, 1941
A beautiful piece of workmanship: the right front wheel steering knuckle, halfshaft, constant-velocity universal-joint (not visible), brake drum, and hub. The brake mechanism worked on the principle of a disc clutch. *GBC ex GRDC*

5 km onward. His highest speed with the blown 183 on No Nox gas was 158.446 mph for the flying-start 5 km.

The two surviving Gulf sixes were extensively rebuilt for the 1941 500. The existing fuel tanks were obviously deadly and had to go. New steel frames were built, with box-section side members which also served as fuel tanks. The bodies were reworked, much to their aesthetic detriment. This time, both cars managed to qualify, albeit very slowly. Then, at 7 a.m. of the morning of the big race, Barringer's crew began fuelling his car. The accepted though tenuous theory of what followed

Miller-Gulf Six, 1941
With their bodies in place, the Gulf sixes looked best from this angle, less graceful from the front. The supercharger intercooler was immense—it must have refrigerated the mixture. *GBC ex GRDC*

93

Miller-Gulf Six, 1941

A chassis under construction; the front suspension and lateral fuel tanks were incomplete. Miller had abandoned his own traditional methods to a large extent, but the front-drive unit bore a strong resemblance to that of the Hepburn car of 1928. *GBC ex GRDC*

is that the gasoline's heavy fumes settled to the ground and found their way to a garage two stalls away. A blowtorch was in use, there was a tremendous boom, and in an instant Barringer's car was on fire. It was a total loss, although the cool-headed driver was able to start the other Gulf six and tool it to safety. Half of one of the long Indy garage buildings was gutted, two other cars were consumed, a pall of dense black smoke hung over the area for hours, and the race got off to a long-delayed start. In it the second Gulf car and sole survivor, driven by Al Miller—no relation to Harry—lasted all of twenty-two laps before its transmission failed.

Indianapolis, 1941
The Miller-Gulf venture ended in flames as clouds of dense black smoke churn above the Indy garage due to the fire that started in the Gulf cars' garages. The results were disastrous as three race cars were destroyed. *IMS*

Then came America's entry into World War II. Soon after that, Gulf disposed of the one remaining Miller car to George Barringer, who promptly sold it to Tucker. It was entered in the 1946 Indianapolis race as the Tucker Torpedo Special, the name of the passenger car which the controversial promoter was preparing to manufacture in large numbers. Driven by Barringer, it lasted a paltry twenty-seven laps at Indy, before retiring with, once more, failure of its temperamental transmission.

The car was entered for the 1947 500, bearing the name Preston Tucker. Al Miller qualified it nineteenth in a field of thirty-three, only to retire on lap 33 with "magneto trouble" whereas the real problem, according to Dees, was that one of the "safer" fuel tanks had sprung a leak. Still promoting the Tucker Torpedo car program, the same machine was entered for Indy again in 1948, when Al Miller put a connecting rod through its crankcase in practice. The car eventually became one of the gems of the Speedway's great Hall of Fame Museum.

Thus ended the Miller-Gulf experiment which had been so full of promise. Even if the cars had run as intended, their better competitors would have run circles around them. What, then, was the meaning of the exercise? ■

Agajanian-Offy, 1953
Developed from Miller's dohc four-cylinder, rebaptized as the Offenhauser, continued the tradition, ruling over all comers for decades in American racing. J. C. Agajanian's number 98 was AAA National Champion for several seasons. *GB*

Chapter Twelve: The Miller-Offenhauser Fours

THE FIRST TWIN-CAM MILLER FOURS to compete in the Indianapolis 500 did so in 1930. There were seven of them and, to universal amazement, one of them finished second, serving notice of a new era to come. The last Offys to run at Indy did so in 1980; having been rendered non-competitive more by fuel-consumption regulations than by mere advanced age. In terms of active life span at the vortex of top-level racing, there is no other prime mover that can begin to approach this record. The Miller four, in its various mutations, is the most successful racing engine of all time.

The Roots of the Miller Dohc Four

In 1926, Dick Loynes of Long Beach was an active competitor in the American Power Boat Association's 151 ci class. Some 151 hydroplanes used modified Duesenberg eights, but the class really was dominated by four-bangers, chiefly Fronty Fords and Stars converted to overhead valves. This was very simply because tight, one-buoy turns were then in use, and the superior low-speed torque of the fours made them much faster in coming out of the turns. The existing engines were at the limit of their development potential and Loynes asked Miller to build him a rugged, lightly stressed twin-cam four from which more power could be extracted, in response to eventual future need. Just a few months before, Miller had extrapolated an 8c, two-valve, 310 ci marine racing engine from his highly successful automotive 122. Goossen drew up one half of the 310, following Loynes' specifications. The little engine turned out to be as rugged as a diesel, had all the acceleration and durability for which the client had hoped, and made him almost unbeatable in both national and international competition. When Loynes' exclusive call on this engine expired the following year, Miller built and sold quantities of marine 151s.

It was following Miller's sale to Schofield, but still during the 1929 racing season, that a bizarre idea occurred to Bill White, a prominent race-car owner and promoter. Watching the performance of the four-cylinder engines in boat racing, it occurred to

Miss California, 1929
The dohc Miller four was first developed for marine use, as in boats such as champion Dick Loynes' *Miss California.*
GBC ex Dick Loynes

Miller Four Specials, 1930
Cars of William S. "Bill" White, who was the first car owner to try a four-cylinder Miller engine at Indy. Number 32 was the Duesenberg that won the 1927 Indy 500; it was later fitted with a Miller 91 engine. Number 3 was the four-cylinder car built and raced by Lou Moore. *GBC ex FU*

(*top*)
Miller Four Dohc, circa 1930
This twin-cam Miller four modeled a beautifully formed prop drive unit, presumably also Miller designed and built. *MR/SM ex TC*

were needed. When we were sure that the engine would stand up under the toughest racing conditions we went up to Muroc Dry Lake for a flat-out speed run. We clocked a record 144.895 mph. We knew then that we had stumbled onto something big and that we were ready for Indy."

That was Bill White's distant recall. Carburetion and cam wizard Ed Winfield recalled other details. "The converted 151 didn't do well enough to beat the best Fords," he said. "So White went to Harry Miller and they decided that they would build a 200 ci four with five main bearings. The boat engine was big and heavy, and they lightened it. They made both eight and 16-valve blocks for it, but White preferred the eight-valve. It did very well, beating just about everything. That was the beginning of the four-cylinder era."

White took his surprise package to the Speedway in 1930. He was greeted with ridicule for trying to compete against the super-refined modern eights with a four which was, by definition, obsolete. But Cantlon scored the third fastest time among the thirty-eight qualifiers and had no trouble holding second place throughout the 500-mile endurance test. He drove the flying four throughout the season and finished in second place in National Championship point standings.

Miller, back in business after his brief retirement, developed an economy racing engine to suit the hard times. It was a four-valve, five main-bearing, 220 ci four. It hardly sold at all and, following his resultant bankruptcy, his company's assets were sold at auction.

The Birth of Offenhauser Engineering

Dick Loynes bought and preserved all of the drawings, patterns, engines, and parts. Offenhauser invested $800, almost all he had, in machine tools. He told me, "It was the most desperate thing I ever

him that what worked on water might work equally well on road and track. He invested in a 151, bored it out to 183, and installed it in a Miller 91. His driver, Shorty Cantlon, came in from his first gallop with the car at Los Angeles' Legion Ascot Speedway, shaking, and said, "My God, Bill—she runs like a wild horse!"

"We ran the car at Ascot every Sunday, working out the bugs," White told me years later. "We had trouble keeping valves, pistons, and wrist pins from failing, but Offenhauser put in long hours with us at the track itself. We figured out what had to be done, and Fred and Leo saw to it that we got the improved parts that

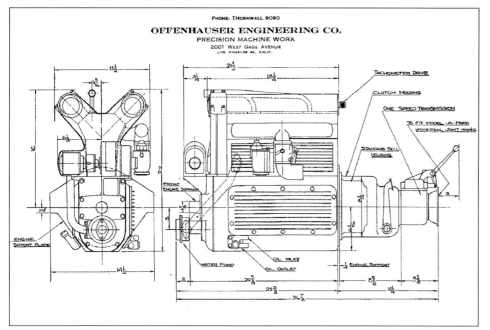

Fred Offenhauser, 1952
Taking it easy at home not long after his retirement—he was convinced the Pekinese brought him good luck. *GB*

(above left)
Offenhauser, 1934
Installation sheet for the new Offy Midget engine. *GBC*

Miller Four 220, 1934
Shorty Cantlon drove the Sullivan-O'Brien Special, powered by a Miller 220 four and built by Myron Stevens, one of the great artisan engineers in the field. *IMS*

(far left)
Offenhauser Factory, 1939
Many Miller alumni made up the crew at Offenhauser's new plant where production of the Miller-Offy commenced. At extreme left, Frank Adamson; at far right, Fred Offenhauser. *GBC ex LG*

(top near left)
Leo Goossen, 1953
Goossen displays a pair of supercharger impellers. The larger one was part of an Offy development program; the smaller one was from a Miller 91. *GB*

(bottom near left)
Offenhauser, 1953
For sports-car use, Offys often were fitted with SU sidedraft carburetors. *GB*

(top far left)
Louis Meyer and Dale Drake, 1954
Meyer, left, and Drake show off a supercharger drive gear, which has a spring-mounted hub to cushion shocks of sudden changes of impeller velocity. *GB*

(bottom far left)
Juan Manuel Fangio, 1954
Fangio, left, spent a week in Los Angeles shopping for an exceptional car with a blown Offy to drive at Indy. Driving the original BRM Formula 1 car had convinced him of the advantages of a good centrifugal supercharger, but the right combination had yet to be discovered. The author, holding the large circular slide rule, was the Argentine champion's interpreter and guide. *Lester Nahamkin*

(near left)
Offenhauser, 1954
The gifted hands of Takeo "Chickie" Hiroshima giving the finishing touches to a supercharger impeller. *GB*

did, but I owed everything I had or was to the racing fraternity. And if I didn't look after their needs, who would?"

Ed Winfield said: "Fred kept the old organization together, and he had the advantage of having men who had worked on the same equipment most of their lives. He didn't make much money until the war came along, but he managed to keep the doors open and pay everybody's wages, which was more than Miller had been able to do. Harry always had too much overhead for the amount of business he was able to conduct. Fred, by cutting all the corners and not having any of the things that you should have in a business, was able to make a success of it."

Anyone could try to build a Miller engine by obtaining the drawings and rough castings through Dick Loynes. There was a long, lean time when there was little action on the four-cylinder front. In 1931, the best four at Indy finished eighth. In 1932, a four finished second again, but the next best was only fourteenth. Then in 1933, fours finished second and third and business began to pick up for the newly named Offenhauser Engineering Company. Fred bought the patterns and drawings for the Miller 255 from Loynes and put his own nameplate on the engines he sold, apparently starting in 1935, when the Offy name begins to appear in Indianapolis records. The engine's real reign, however, began the year before. Thirteen Miller fours were entered in the 500, and they finished one, two, three, four, nine, and eleven. The two-valve Offy Midget was created, to a certain extent, in Offenhauser's shop in 1934. According to Winfield, it was developed around one cylinder block of the Hartz-Miller 8c 182, which itself was an enlarged 8c 122. And in 1937 Fred bored and stroked the 255 to create the 270, to take full advantage of the 4.5 liter displacement limit.

Business was beginning to pick up nicely when the United States entered World War II. Offenhauser's precision machine shop was discovered by the local aircraft industry, and he and it worked around the clock, seven days a week, for the duration. Feeling his 68 years in 1946, he decided to sell, but only to someone who would carry on the tradition and care in a responsible manner for its clientele. He found the ideal combination in his friends Louis Meyer and Dale Drake, both ex-racing men and both with good backgrounds in manufacturing.

The Meyer & Drake Offenhauser Engine
With the purchase they inherited the highly expert staff, including the incomparable services of designer Leo Goossen. The nameplates that identified their product read, "Offenhauser Engine, made by Meyer & Drake Engineering."

The Offy lived its age of greatest glory under Meyer & Drake. Between 1947 and 1965 it won the 500 every year. Between 1949 and 1962 at least nine of the top ten finishers were Offys but usually all ten were of the same marque. In eleven of those races, every one of the thirty-three starters was Offy-powered. Naturally there were those who grumbled about this state of affairs, while many observers saw this as giving all contestants equal weapons, thereby sharpening the focus on individual ability to drive, to tune like engines, and to build and set up chassis.

The Offy's fantastic long reign was broken in 1965 by the recently introduced Ford four-camshaft v-8. Ironically, Meyer & Drake made such specialized parts as the cam-follower cups for the new Ford racing engine and also had become its official sales agent. Following the Ford victory at Indy, Louis Meyer sold his interest in their company to Dale Drake and moved to Indianapolis, to work directly with the Ford racing division. Drake, convinced that the Offy would rise again, carried on, with Leo Goossen still at his side. The only hope of overtaking the new four-cam Ford lay in supercharging.

As far back as 1949 the iron horse that was the Offy had been considered to be at the end of its tether. The regulations that were in effect governing American Championship racing at that

(*above*)

Miller Four Dohc, circa 1955

Infinite questions concerning the construction of Miller-family engines can be answered by this photo of the components of an Offy 270, taken in the Miller & Drake factory in the early 1950s. Walt Sobraske, left, began working for Miller in 1921; Takeo Hiroshima in the mid-1930s. *GBC ex LG*

(near left)

Offenhauser 180, 1954

Louis Meyer of Meyer & Drake, aided by Meyer's son, left, and George Salih, right, with an Offy 180 on the dyno. The centrifugal blower is of in-house, Leo Goossen, design and manufacture. *GB*

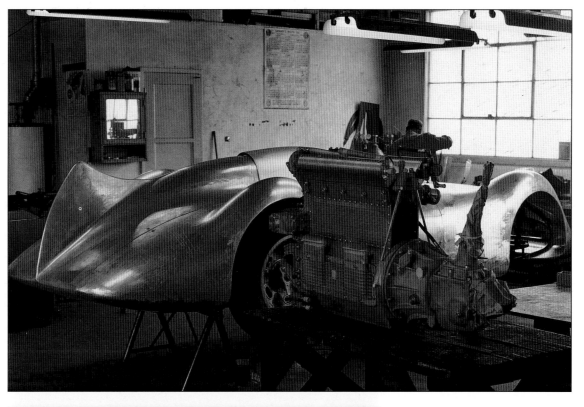

(near left)

Offenhauser, 1955

The builders of Indy roadsters began tilting their Offy engines, then laid them flat, to lower their cars' centers of gravity. *GB*

(near left)

Offenhauser, circa 1955

All Miller-family engines had cylinder heads that were an integral part of the cylinder block. Some had two valves per cylinder, some four. This is an Offy 270. *GBC*

(above)

Offenhauser 270, circa 1955

A fresh Offy awaiting installation in the Kurtis Kraft plant. The inclined steel rods at the rear of this fuel injected 270 Offy engine had been added to the design to help keep the cylinder block from tearing itself off of the crankcase. *GB*

(far left)

Offenhauser, circa 1958

Further experiments with supercharging the small Offy involved the use of intercoolers, again created in-house. *GBC ex LG*

(left)

Offenhauser, circa 1955

Inside the barrel crankcase there were bulkheads, integral with the light-alloy casting, to which the bronze main-bearing supports were mounted. *GBC*

103

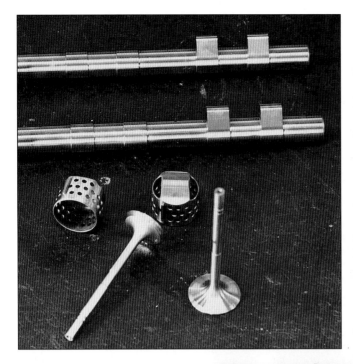

(*above*)
Offenhauser, circa 1955
Although there are exceptions, almost all twin-cam engines devote one camshaft to the inlet valves and the other to the exhausts. This permits varying the timing of one set of valves without touching that of the other set. One of the famous cup-type cam followers is here, well lightened. *GB*

(*above right*)
Offenhauser, circa 1955
Like most Offys, the 270 had five main bearings. In the foreground are the bronze diaphragms that gave them 360-degree support. *GB*

Offenhauser 171, 1957
In search of a new winning combination, the Offy 171 was equipped with a Roots supercharger in 1957. *GBC ex LG*

time limited normally aspirated engines to 4.5 liters, 274.5 ci and those supercharged to three liter, 183 ci. The centrifugally supercharged Offy 176 was developed to give a potent 460 bhp at 6500 rpm, which promised to give the vintage engine a new lease on life. Three cars so equipped qualified for the 500 in 1950, but none went the distance. The unblown 270 charged on until 1957, when the displacement limit was reduced to 171 ci blown and 255 ci unblown. A sole blown Offy, driven by Rodger Ward, lasted only twenty-seven laps at Indianapolis, when put out by supercharger bearing failure. Still, blowing remained the key to vast additional output and certain specialists, notably Herb Porter, Dick Jones, and Stuart Hilborn, continued to work on the problem. It was fortunate that they did, because the Ford-induced crisis of 1965 left Drake Engineering with two alternatives: master supercharging, or close its doors. To benefit from the former, one would have to be able to turn the engine far faster than ever before; the engine would have to be redesigned. Dale Drake decided to take that costly course and gave Leo Goossen the green light.

The Revised Offenhauser and DGS

Leo had just celebrated his 70th birthday when he undertook this, one of the landmark jobs of his long career. The essential task was to shorten the engine's stroke greatly, in order to achieve much higher rpm. He reduced the stroke of the previous 176 by 0.625 in, arriving at 3.125 in. This, with a bore of 4.125 in, gave a displacement of 167 ci, although the engine was called the 168. The 72-degree valve-included angle and traditional siamesed ports were left unchanged, and the revised Offy was complete in late October of that year. This is the engine to which Porter, Hilborn, and Bob DeBisschop of AiResearch applied one of that firm's turbochargers to arrive, by painstaking stages, at earth-shaking results. In 1966 the best finish by a turbocharged Offy at Indianapolis was eighth place; the top four finishers were Fords. In 1967, seven of the eight qualifying Offys were turbos, but only two finished the race, seventh and eighth. Ford took the top five places. And then in 1968 the successful combination was cracked, with turbo Offys filling nine of the top eleven places, and Bobby Unser winning the 500.

In 1969, the displacement limit was reduced to 161.0 ci, which brought the Offy's bore to 4.13 in and swept volume to 159.5. Fords won that year at Indianapolis and in the two years that followed, the best turbo Offy being third in '69 and '70 and second in '71. Then, in '72, the Offys finally hit their stride, sweeping the top three places that year and the year after. In 1975 and 1976, first place was theirs again. Then in 1977, the best Offy was fourth and in 1978, third. That was the year that Cosworth first won at Indy—a truly modern engine that opened a new era in motor racing in which no four-banger could survive.

There was a last and very promising mutation in the Offy design tradition called the DGS for Drake-Goossen-Sparks. Art Sparks, a racing personage of many talents, was very much in tune with the times concerning valve-included angle, combustion-chamber, and piston design when, in 1973, he interested car owner Pat

Patrick and his chief mechanic George Bignotti in a redesign of the existing Offy. They persuaded Dale Drake to permit Sparks to work with Goossen on such a project. Art narrowed the valve-included angle drastically to 44 degrees, transformed the combustion chamber and piston crown, and separated the historically siamesed two-valve ports, creating smoother passages. While this project was in progress, Leo Goossen died in 1974, at the age of 79, by far the greatest designer of racing machinery that the United States ever produced. That he died with his boots on, so to speak, is the way he would have wanted it to be.

According to Sparks, about twelve DGS engines were produced by Drake. They showed great promise, but wrought no wonders before the Cosworths arrived. Dale Drake had the last word when, in 1975, he again redesigned the Offy to have a stroke of only 2.65 in and a valve-included angle of just 38 degrees. About twenty-four were produced before Drake Engineering closed its doors for good in December 1979, laying the long-evergreen Miller four to rest at last. ∎

Offenhauser 168, 1966
The AiResearch exhaust-gas driven turbocharger was applied to the Offy 168 in 1966. The consequences were what we have witnessed since: earth-shaking.
GBC ex LG

Chapter Thirteen: Last Days in Detroit

Miller 91 Front-Drive, 1928
On the Packard test track at Ithica, Michigan, on June 14, 1928, Leon Duray drove his front-drive Miller 91 to a new International Class and World Record on a closed circuit: an average of 148.17 mph for 2.5 miles. The record stood for twenty-four years. *GBC ex Packard Motor Car Co. Archives*

HE SOJOURN WITH GULF had its familial compensations. Edna's parents lived near Schenley Park in Pittsburgh, and their daughter and son-in-law found an apartment nearby them. But it would not have been in character for Harry to remain in that backwater—relative to his interests—any longer than it took to arrive at the essentially definitive form of the Gulf six. It had been a richly instructive experience, which had included the development of the engine which had started out as the aero 255. I assume that he never had any doubts about the Gulf venture as a viable racing effort. He certainly knew that World War II was about to erupt, putting an end to racing for its duration.

The industrial establishment of Hitler's Third Reich had embarked upon a very active program of recruitment among engineers and technicians of German extraction who worked in the United States and possessed knowledge of American methods and skills. Edna told me that her husband had received very liberal inducements to bring his experience to Germany, but they did not appeal to him. He was born an American, had become part of the fabric of American life, and would stay around if the going got rough.

It was in the spring of 1939, Eddie Offutt told me, that Harry left Gulf, with instructions to Offutt as to how he believed the car program should be carried on. He moved to Indianapolis, where he was among many old friends, and set up a small engineering business. There he worked with the Kermath Manufacturing Company of Detroit on the design of a supercharged 1725 ci engine, to be used in high-speed patrol boats. His main undertaking during this period of a little over one year was the design of a twin-cam engine for pursuit planes, in both v-12 and v-16 versions, for Bell Aircraft. He was aided, again, by his faithful engineering draftsman, Everett Stevenson. At this stage of his career, Miller had become convinced of the virtues of camshaft drive by means of a central gear train, in the manner of the Alfa Romeo eights of Vittorio Jano. It is opportune to note here that Miller was one of the few engine designers in the world who, along with Ettore Bugatti, Louis Coatalen, and Louis and Arthur Chevrolet, ever considered dual overhead camshafts to be compatible with aero-engine use. Miller is said to have used central camshaft drive in his studies for Bell, of which no traces seem to remain. Certainly, the engines were never built.

Whatever Miller's feeling may have been about Tucker as a result of the Ford Indianapolis fiasco of 1935, he lost very little time in renewing serious business relations with this operator who sought to make Washington his beat. On December 15, 1939, Tucker's American Aero Marine Corporation (in process of formation), in conjunction with the Tucker Manufacturing Company of Detroit, sent to the Navy's Chief of the Bureau of Aeronautics a detailed proposal for the construction of two large experimental engines. The job would cost the Navy a round $100,000 and, above the signatures of Preston Tucker and Harry Miller, the proposal ended with, "We would like to start construction January 1, 1940."

This project was still alive on June 24, 1940, when Miller telegraphed certain modifications to the Bureau. Then, on October 24, Tucker wrote to William Knudsen of the National Defense Commission. He stated that his firm had received a contract from the Navy for the two large engines, plus another from the Army for an airplane and four engines for it. The letter specified that the basic engine was "a straight-eight and actually a copy of our Miller 255." The letter, on the stationery of a newcomer, the Tucker Aircraft Corporation, acknowledged serious financial difficulties and accused the Navy and Army of bad pay.

The Rosen Papers also contain a Bureau of Aeronautics inter-office memo dated December 4, 1940, and titled "Memorandum of Visit—Lafland Miller 255 ci Engine." It states, "The engine is somewhat similar to the 6-cylinder Miller engine now under development at Gulf. . . ." The role of Mr. Lafland is defined as having been the introduction of austenitic valve seats; otherwise the engine was "a typical Miller design." It was too late for it to fit into the training-plane program, for

which it was ineligible for a number of other reasons. In conclusion, one of the experts participating said that he "saw no way in which the engine could be employed advantageously in the Navy except probably for motor boat use by the Bureau of Ships."

There were other projects which were masterminded by Tucker. All ended badly, and it was already in August 1940, that Miller walked away from his chief engineer's position, tired of working without being paid. He moved to Detroit.

He rented a modest shop at 229 Walker Street, at the corner of Wight. He named his new business the Miller Engine Works, Inc., not just in memory of the good old days in far-away Los Angeles, but because he had every intention of returning to the love of his life, engine building, as soon as conditions should permit. But for the here and now he chose to become a "maker of aircraft test fixtures for hydraulic actuating cylinders and circuits for landing gear, of aircraft wing flaps, cowl flaps, brakes, bomb-bay doors, gun turrets; also maker of machine tools and testing devices for indexing, feeding, lifting and power circuits or any combination thereof." This choice of specialization seemed to be a wise and realistic one, but it is not easy to start from scratch when you are 65, have suffered from diabetes for years, have now acquired cancer, and are beginning to need a lot of rest. Miller also did job work for other firms. His business stayed afloat, but it was not an easy life.

As in the old days, this Miller Engine Works was a gathering place for old friends of the racing milieu. One of these was engineer Eddie Offutt, who had also come to work in the Motor City. He was like a loyal son to Miller, and aided him in his projects. In 1952, he described to me the sports car that Miller, ten years earlier, was designing for production when the war would end. It had a six-cylinder twin-cam engine that would develop around 100 bhp. The engine was mounted transversely, ahead of the driven front wheels, and tilted backwards at an angle of 45 degrees, all to aid the bite of the driving wheels when accelerating

NAVY DEPARTMENT
BUREAU OF ENGINEERING
WASHINGTON, D. C.

ENCLOSURES

15 February, 1940.

MEMORANDUM to: Mr. C. S. Fliedner,
Engine Section,
Bureau of Aeronautics.

Subject: Investigation of Facilities of Mr. Preston Tucker and Mr. Harry Miller.

1. Several months ago Mr. Preston Tucker and Mr. Harry Miller made an appointment with me to discuss the construction of 1200 horsepower engines for motor torpedo boats. These engines were to be of very light weight and were to be designed by Mr. Miller, whose fame as a racing automobile designer is well known in this country and in Europe.

2. The conversation sounded most interesting and an interview with Captain Irish was arranged, during which it was decided that I should make a trip to Detroit to determine the facilities available for building these engines.

3. On this trip, I visited the office, which consists of a small unused space over a rather antique machine shop where I met several of the associates of these two gentlemen, who did not impress me too favorably, and in further discussion with Mr. Tucker and Mr. Miller, I became convinced that the proposition which they made was purely a pipe dream.

4. My reaction to the entire conversation is that they have practically no facilities whatsoever and that they are endeavoring in any manner possible to sell the name of Mr. Miller, who appeared to me to be in very poor health, and the possibility of building engines as described by them appeared very remote.

5. Upon my return to Washington I reported to Captain Irish my reaction to the setup and recommended against the conclusion of a contract for engines with Mr. Tucker or Mr. Miller, which recommendation has been followed, to date.

John J. Crane

or mounting a slope. The car was to weigh between 1,600 and 1,800 lb, would have a hydraulic coupling and an automatic transmission of Miller design, which Offutt considered to be as good as those that were being made in the early Fifties. Miller had already built many of the elements in prototype form. He of course was diligently creating a sort of super-Mini Cooper a couple of decades in advance of events. Offutt said, "He was a man who always could see so much farther into the future."

Harry Arminius Miller died in Detroit on May 3, 1943, aged 67. His son Ted, following his wishes, had his body cremated and his ashes placed in a crypt at Forest Lawn Cemetery in Los Angeles, his town. While he was president of the Speedway, three-time Indy winner Wilbur Shaw told me:

"To a great many people, Harry Miller was somewhat of a genius. Although his artistic touch often sacrificed dependability in order to obtain the symmetry and beauty of line that always has distinguished his products from those of any other designer, he achieved world-wide recognition for the creation of efficient internal combustion engines. His lack of a formal engineering background was offset by his honesty and integrity, which invariably outweighed sound economic principles when any question was raised concerning his product. Everything he produced was expected to deliver exactly as he said it would; and he invariably did everything possible to make it so—often to his financial disadvantage. The thoroughbred engines and vehicles he created dominated the motor sports field for almost a generation. He was loved and respected by all who knew him." ∎

(*above*)
Navy Department Report, 1940
An internal report on the facilities of Tucker and Miller, who wanted to sell engines to the American Armed Forces. *GBC ex MR*

(*left*)
Preston Tucker Letter, 1939
Letter from Tucker to the Navy Department concerning a Miller-Tucker joint venture to build 3000 hp aero engines. *GBC ex MR*

Miller 91 Front-Drive, 1927

Leon Duray at the wheel of his front-drive
Miller 91. This car was to become the
Packard Cable Special number 21.

GBC ex Leon Duray

Epilogue: **The Packard Cable Specials**

Packard Cable Special, 1992
The Smithsonian Miller 91 front-drive after its recent restoration by Christopher Leydon. When Borgeson finished his original restoration of the Hepburn car, it was placed on exhibit first in the Los Angeles County Museum, then at the New York Auto Show in 1961, and then was placed in the great Briggs Cunningham Museum near Los Angeles. It was later sold to Bill Harrah before being bought by Robert M. Rubin, who donated the Miller to the Smithsonian Institution in 1992.
Jeff Tinsley

Two of the Packard Cable Specials are of special interest, first of all because of the total of eleven or possibly twelve front-drives built by Miller, these are the only ones that survive in their strictly original form. Second, both are perfectly restored and accessible to the general public today. One is in the Hall of Fame Museum of the Indianapolis Motor Speedway; the other resides at the National Museum of American History of the Smithsonian Institution in Washington DC.

The Indianapolis Museum car was the sixth Miller front-wheel-drive built. It was delivered to famous driver Leon Duray in the summer of 1926. It was painted black, with white frame and wheels, and fitted with a distinctive supercharger intercooler of Duray's own design. Working in close liaison with Harry Miller, Duray was the great early experimenter with methanol (wood alcohol) as an engine fuel; his track tests with it usually were made with this car.

Although Duray never won the Indianapolis 500, he was an extremely fast driver and the holder of many records. On the Culver City boardtrack speedway in 1927, he drove this car to an absolute record for 250 miles of 124.7 mph. The following year at Indianapolis, he set the lap record at 124 mph on the old brick surface without the later banked turns. This record remained unbroken for nine years, the longest ever. Two weeks later, on the banked concrete Packard test track at Utica, Michigan, Duray clocked 142.21 mph for one 2.5-mile lap.

The eleventh Miller front-wheel-drive was completed in 1928, in time to be driven by Ralph Hepburn in that year's Memorial Day 500. It bristled with improvements, including a wider, lower radiator and wider front brake drums, and was called the '28 Series front-drive. Hepburn qualified the beautiful machine in sixth place at Indy, but dropped out on lap 48 with timing-gear failure. Nor was the rest of the season particularly better.

The fate of this car is unknown; Mark Dees and I are of accord that the penultimate and last of the front-wheel-drive Miller 91s were possibly the same car, to which

Miller 91 Front-Drive, 1928

This 1928 car was almost certainly the last Miller front-drive to be built. It was driven at Indy by Ralph Hepburn for owner Harry Miller. He was one of the fastest qualifiers at over 116 mph, but did not finished due to a timing-gear failure. The unique oil tank/cooler also served to receive bumps. Because of its combined fragility and exposed position it may have been deleted from the car as it was not seen again. This is believed to be the car that Hepburn and Duray drove in 1929 as Packard Cable Special number 18. *IMS*

Packard Cable Special, 1929

Duray in Paris, on his way to take part in the Grand Prix of Monza, as the Italian GP was called that year. He is seen here with number 18, the Smithsonian Institution car. Duray drove it to a number of new International Class Records at Montlhéry, near Paris. *GBC ex T.A.S.O. Mathieson*

a number of obvious modifications had been made.

This car, too, passed to Duray, who equipped it with one of his own intercoolers, and with what seems to have been a different version of the 91 engine. Significant, perhaps, is the fact that Duray engaged—or re-engaged—Hepburn to drive the car. The two cars, plus a rear-drive 122 fitted with a 91 engine assigned to Tony Gulotta, were painted violet, with yellow frames and wheels, and ran as Packard Cable Specials, named for a General Motors division which then and now manufactures automotive electrical wiring. Duray and Hepburn qualified in second and third positions for the 1929 Indy 500, but neither lasted the distance.

Next came a complex series of operations on Duray's part, the exact details of which are unlikely ever to be known. First, the GP of Italy had been replaced by the free-formula GP of Monza, to be held in three heats on September 15, 1929. The organizer, Count Vincenzo Florio, liked spectacular American talent and invited Duray to take part—with appearance money, of course. Second, on his way to Monza, Duray decided to pass by Paris and tear off a few record runs locally, thereafter exhibiting the two front-drives for paid admission. Third, he promoted a brand-new L-29 Cord convertible coupe for this expedition. As native guides, he took with him super mechanic Jean Marcenac and the son of French driver Albert Guyot. The son, André, had been working at GM's AC Spark Plug Division on the supercharging of passenger cars. AC, he later told me, owned a pair of Miller rear-drives and a pair of front-drives.

Duray's record attempts at Linas-Montlhéry and Arpajon, near Paris, went well. He was perhaps saving his trusty old 1926 car for Monza, because all of the photos that I have seen from these sessions show No. 18, the "Hepburn" car, in action. On August 25, he set a new International 1500 cc record of 131.73 mph for one mile and 143.3 for 1 km. On September 1, he set new records of 139.22 for 5 miles and 139.55 for 5 km.

Marcenac proceeded with the two Millers by truck for Monza. There, Florio got all the spectacle he had hoped for, and then some, as Duray used

American dirt-track technique to set new lap records and terrorize the natives with both cars before the Millers gave up, each one on a different heat. But everyone was impressed, including Ettore Bugatti, who made a deal on the spot and took the two Millers home. Ettore Bugatti's son Roland told me years later that his father's interest in front-drive was based on his intention to build four-wheel-drive vehicles, which Miller was working on at the same moment. Miller's experiments were satisfying; Bugatti's were not. But Ettore Bugatti did derive great benefit by copying the Miller engine's top end.

Bugatti did nothing to alter the Packard Cable Specials, while their American counterparts continued to race and were updated, mechanically and in bodywork, each season. In 1954, I saw photos of the two cars, covered with dust and lacking engines, in the Bugatti factory. I began negotiating for their purchase from my base in California. It was not until 1959, after an inspection of the cars by friend Bob Estes and telephoned interventions on my behalf by friend Marcenac , that an accord was reached, and I received the cars back in the city of their birth.

Packard Cable Special, 1954
The two Packard Cable Special Miller 91 front-drives were acquired by Ettore Bugatti from Duray after the Monza race. This was how they were found in the Bugatti factory in France in 1954 by Danish diplomat Ditlev Scheel. *GBC ex Ditlev Scheel*

Packard Cable Special, 1959

Griffith Borgeson bought the two Packard Cable Specials from Bugatti. Here the future Smithsonian car was being pushed out of its crate at Los Angeles Harbor by Borgeson, left, and his friend Jean Marcenac, right. Marcenac had come to the United States in 1919 with the Ballot team, was chief mechanic to Frank Lockhart, then Duray, for whom he took the Packard Cable cars to Europe. He aided the author in his acquisition of the cars from Bugatti and in their repatriation in 1959 when he still reigned over the immortal front-drive Novi racing cars—pure Miller descendants.

GBC ex Wayne Thoms

As I was fully aware of their rarity and historic value, I felt that they belonged in the Smithsonian and in the museum of the Indianapolis Speedway, whose owner, Tony Hulman, called me before I had time to contact him, asking what it would take to get the original Duray car. I told him that it was his, but that it would be nice if he would reimburse the pittance that Bugatti had charged me for these derelicts. No problem. When I contacted the Smithsonian, I learned that they had no collection plan for old racing cars at that time. Therefore, I was left with the last and most perfected of the Miller front-drives, to dismantle with loving care and explore Miller and Duray's secrets.

Aside from the painting and plating (all nickel on copper), I jealously kept all of the work to myself. When I found that one rod and piston assembly was missing and that the cast-aluminum-alloy transaxle housing was gravely cracked, I realized that a fully operational restoration was beyond my means. I completed the cosmetic transformation and placed the car, on loan, first in the Los Angeles County Museum and then in the vast collection of thoroughbreds that Briggs Cunningham had assembled with such taste and care. In 1969, Bill Harrah of Reno offered me $25,000 for the machine. It was an eminently fair price for the time, and the car passed to him.

The car spent a long time in the Harrah shops, where it was made to run and, out of good intentions, the body colors were reversed from the scheme they bore when found in the Bugatti plant. After that great collector's death in 1978, his staggering assemblage of machines remained in limbo for several years. A large percentage of them, including the Miller, passed in 1986 to General William Lyon.

A few years later, Robert M. Rubin, a young financier, purchased the Miller from him. He turned it over to expert Christopher Leydon for total re-restoration. Perhaps even better than new in 1991, running like a watch and screaming like a purebred banshee, the last of the 91 front-drives brought the sound and substance of Miller tradition back to life at Bridgehampton and at Laguna Seca. Rubin also showed this prize at the annual lavish concours at Bagatelle in Paris' Bois de Boulogne.

Packard Cable Special, 1959
Borgeson reads one of the Duray car's plugs as Customs Examiner Melvin Bowden verifies that the import was of American origin. Beyond that, it had returned to its hometown.
GBC ex Los Angeles Herald-Express

Packard Cable Special, circa 1960
Borgeson gave the Duray car to the
Indianapolis Speedway Museum, where it
may be seen today. Restoration was done
by the museum staff. *IMS*

This spectacular renaissance of an all-too-for-
gotten masterpiece happened to coincide with new
developments at the Smithsonian Institution.
There, in the Transportation Division of the
National Museum of American History, auto racing expert Gordon E. White, aided by curator
William L. Withuhn, had conceived and developed a collection plan for historic American racing cars. At the top of their list was a representative Miller.

White was not sure how many authentic
Millers survived, and he spent a good year re-
searching the question among his contacts all over
the country. The ex-Harrah/Lyon car had dropped
totally out of sight, until well-known automotive
historian Richard F. Merritt provided the clue that
led White to Christopher Leydon's scientific laboratory of a shop in Lahaska, Pennsylvania. He
arrived at that point in the story when old Number 18 was in pieces, undergoing revision and
restoration from the ground up.

It so happened that Leydon's father—Rear
Admiral John K. Leydon— already had close asso-
ciations with the Smithsonian, which made White
a particularly welcome visitor. Learning the iden-
tity of the car's owner, White promptly contacted
Rubin who, at that time, was interested not in
museum talk, but in getting his historic front-drive
91 flashing around racing circuits again.

When Leydon's restoration was completed
there was no doubt in White's mind that this was
the car that the Smithsonian should have. Rubin
was persuaded to meet with museum officials and
the idea of his donating the car to the nation was
launched. Four months went by, while both he and
the museum pondered the matter. The museum
engaged experts from the world's leading auction
houses to appraise the car. This was after the price
crash of 1991, but estimates of its current market
value ran as high as $5 million—quite a bit to give
away.

However, Rubin knew that his car was a
national treasure and he liked the idea of it join-
ing the Wright Flyer and the first American probes
of outer space. Rubin expressed certain desires,
among them that the Miller should not be interred
in the museum in perpetuity, but instead should be
taken out from time to time and allowed to stretch
its sinews and howl, for purposes of cultural edifi-
cation. To implement this he posted a $100,000
endowment for the Transportation Division. He
named the endowment for his father, Harold
Rubin, a retired school teacher of mechanical arts.
The accord finally reached gave Robert Rubin, in
partial exchange for the Miller, an early Mercedes.

On Christmas Eve 1991, one absolutely pristine front-wheel-drive Miller 91 took up residence
in a museum storage building, to await its official
installation. That event occurred on April 23,
1992, when glistening Number 18 took its place in
the nation's most distinguished showcase for historic artifacts. I had the privilege of being there,
along with the museum's directors, Robert Rubin
and his parents, and a fascinating array of guests.
Everyone felt that the car had found its proper
home. ∎

Appendix I: Miller Engine Specifications

Year	Type	Cyl.	Bore (in)	Stroke (in)	Disp. (ci)	Disp. (lit)	CR	BHP	RPM	Valves /Cyl.	In. Valve Dia. (in)	VIA (Deg)	Main Brngs.	S/C	S/B Ratio	MPS (ft/min)	BHP/L	BMEP (psi)	MGV (ft/sec)	Weight (lb/kg)
1915	Burman-Peugeot	4	3.63	7.10	293.11	4.80	na	100	3000	4	2.00	60	3	na	1.96	3550	20.82	90	97	511/232
1915	Christofferson Aero	6	4.75	6.00	637.94	10.45	na	120	1400	2	2.37	na	na	na	1.26	1400	11.48	106	94	na
1917	289 Auto 300	4	3.63	7.00	288.98	4.74	na	155	2900	4	2.00	30	na	na	1.93	3383	32.73	146	93	450/204
1917	352 Aero	4	4.00	7.00	351.86	5.77	na	155	2900	4	2.00	na	na	na	1.75	3383	26.88	120	113	410/186
1917	V-12 Aero, 60-degreeV	12	5.00	6.00	1413.72	23.17	na	400	1600	2	2.50	na	na	na	1.20	1600	17.27	140	107	na
1919	Baby Chevrolet	4	3.09	6.00	180.44	2.96	na	na	na	4	na	na	na	na	1.94	na	na	na	na	na
1920	TNT/T4	4	3.38	5.00	178.92	2.93	6.70	na	na	4	na	60	3	na	1.48	na	na	na	na	na
1922	Leach 999 passenger car	6	3.75	5.25	347.91	5.70	na	na	na	2	1.94	na	4	na	1.40	na	na	na	na	na
1921	183	8	2.69	4.00	181.59	2.98	7.25	125	4000	2	1.25	50	3	na	1.49	2667	42.01	136	103	na
1923	183/12	8	2.53	3.00	120.75	1.98	7.25	105	4500	2	1.25	50	3	na	1.19	2250	53.05	153	77	na
1923	122	8	2.33	3.50	119.39	1.96	7.50	120	5000	2	1.31	98	5	na	1.50	2917	61.13	159	154	na
1925	122 S/C	8	2.33	3.50	119.39	1.96	7.00	203	5800	2	1.31	98	5	C	1.50	3383	103.41	231	179	na
1926	91	8	2.19	3.00	90.16	1.48	6.25	154	7000	2	1.19	94	5	C	1.37	3500	104.24	193	197	na
1926	310 Marine	8	3.41	4.25	309.78	5.08	7.00	200	3500	2	na	86	9	na	1.25	2479	39.40	146	na	880/399
1926	151 Marine	4	3.41	4.25	154.89	2.54	na	95	3500	2	na	86	5	C*	1.25	2479	37.43	139	na	440/200
1926	620 Marine, 60-degreeV	16	3.41	4.25	619.57	10.15	na	425	3500	2	na	86	9	na	1.25	2479	41.86	155	na	1225/556
1927	Lockhart 91	8	2.19	3.00	90.16	1.48	na	285	8000	2	1.19	94	5	C	1.37	4000	192.91	313	225	na
1930	Chancellor 310, 47-degreeV	8	3.41	4.25	309.78	5.08	na	325	na	2	na	86	5	C	1.25	na	64.02	na	na	1225/556
1928	148 Flat 8	8	2.59	3.50	147.97	2.42	na	260	6000	2	na	90	na	C	1.35	3500	107.22	232	na	na
1929	3300 W-24	24	5.00	7.00	3298.67	54.06	na	1500	2600	2	na	30	9	na	1.40	3033	27.75	139	na	na
1930	DO Cragar Ford A	4	4.00	4.13	207.34	3.40	na	175	4800	2	na	60	3	na	1.03	3300	51.50	139	na	na
1930	Miller-Schofield 183	4	3.75	4.25	187.76	3.08	9.70	185	5000	2	na	86	5	na	1.13	3542	60.13	156	na	na
1931	230 Big Eight	8	3.13	3.75	230.10	3.77	11.50	230	6000	2	1.75	na	5	na	1.20	3750	61.00	132	199	na
1931	303 V-16, 45-degreeV	16	2.63	3.50	303.07	4.97	11.00	300	6000	2	1.31	na	7	na	1.33	3500	60.41	131	234	618/280
1931	200	4	3.88	4.25	200.48	3.29	na	190	5000	4	1.50	72	5	na	1.10	3542	57.83	150	197	325/147
1932	220	4	4.06	4.25	220.36	3.61	na	250	6000	4	1.50	72	5	na	1.05	4250	69.23	150	260	325/147
1931	1113 V-16 Marine, 54-degreeV	16	4.44	4.50	1113.52	18.25	na	1800	6000	4	1.69	na	9	2R	1.01	4500	98.53	213	259	1635/743
1932	308 V-8, 45-degreeV	8	3.50	4.00	307.88	5.05	10.50	400	6500	2	1.89	80	5	na	1.14	4333	59.46	119	248	na
1932	182 8C Hartz	8	2.88	3.50	181.77	2.98	na	na	na	2	1.37	90	5	na	1.22	na	na	na	na	na
1933	Miller-Gulf four 255	4	4.25	4.50	255.35	4.18	na	250	5000	4	1.56	72	5	na	1.06	3750	59.74	155	232	485/220
1934	Offenhauser Midget	4	2.97	3.50	96.93	1.59	na	90	6500	2	1.44	90	3	na	1.18	3792	56.66	113	269	230/104
1937	Offenhauser 270	4	4.31	4.63	269.91	4.42	na	240	5000	4	1.72	72	5	na	1.07	3854	54.26	141	202	na
1938	Miller-Gulf six	6	3.50	3.13	180.40	2.96	5.50	246	4600	2	na	90	7	C	0.89	2396	83.22	235	na	na
1949	Offenhauser 176	4	3.88	3.75	176.90	2.90	na	460	6500	4	1.50	72	5	C	0.97	4063	158.68	317	226	na
1953	Offenhauser Sports 91	4	3.00	3.13	88.36	1.45	na	125	7000	2	1.50	90	5	na	1.04	3646	86.33	160	243	na
1954	Offenhauser 180	4	3.97	3.63	179.04	2.93	na	5.75	6000	4	1.50	72	5	C	0.91	3625	195.98	424	211	na
1954	Offenhauser 270	4	4.28	4.63	266.29	4.36	na	330	5000	4	1.72	72	5	na	1.08	3854	75.62	196	256	na
1955	Offenhauser Sports 180	4	3.97	3.63	179.04	2.93	na	220	na	na	na	72	5	na	0.91	na	74.99	na	na	na
1957	Offenhauser 255	4	4.28	4.38	251.89	4.13	na	410	6700	4	1.71	72	5	na	1.02	4885	99.33	192	255	na
1952	Offenhauser 255	4	4.28	4.38	251.89	4.13	14.00	400	6700	4	1.71	72	5	na	1.02	4885	96.90	188	256	na
1966	Offenhauser 168 R	4	4.13	3.13	167.05	2.74	na	525	8500	4	na	72	5	R	0.76	4427	191.78	293	na	na
1966	Offenhauser 168 T	4	4.13	3.13	167.05	2.74	na	625	8500	4	na	72	5	T	0.76	4427	228.31	349	na	na
1969	Offenhauser 159 T	4	4.03	3.13	159.52	2.61	na	700	8500	4	1.56	72	5	T	0.78	4427	267.78	409	246	na
1974	Offenhauser 159 DGS	4	4.03	3.13	159.52	2.61	na	900	9000	4	na	44	5	T	0.78	4688	344.28	296	na	na
1975	Offenhauser 159 DGS	4	4.38	2.65	159.35	2.61	na	829	9000	4	1.65	38	5	T	0.61	3975	317.47	458	233	na

Notes: Mean Gas Velocity (MGV) by Brian Lovell. *Optional. VIA (Deg) means Valve Included Angle. MPS (ft/min) means Mean Piston Speed.

Appendix II: Comprehensive Specifications of the Miller 91

Engine

Cylinders.......................................Eight
Bore x Stroke................................2.1875x3.0in, 55.54x76.20mm
Displacement ....90.2ci, 1478 cc
Valve port diameter 1.4375in
Valve diameter
      Inlet 1.25in
      Exhaust 1.1875in
Valves per cylinder......................Two
Valve included angle ....94 degrees
Valve timing ....5–38–35–8 degrees
Valve lift 0.34375in
Camshafts....................................Two, overhead
Camshaft bearings ....Ten each, steel on aluminum
Camshaft drive.............................Spur-gear train on ball bearings
Valve spring pressure..................Closed 87lb; Open 110lb
Cam followers ....Piston type, radiussed and keyed
Connecting rod type....................Tubular, two cap bolts
Connecting rod bearings.............Poured in rods
Bearing diameter & width.............1.6875x1.34375in
Bearing clearance........................0.0025in
Piston type ....Aluminum, solid skirt
Piston rings..................................Two compression, one oil
Piston diameter 2.180in
Skirt-to-wall clearance 0.006–0.008in
Wrist-pin bushing ....Steel
Wrist-pins retained by.................Aluminum buttons
Crankshaft type ....Four-four, counterbalanced
Firing order 1–5–3–7–4–8–2–6
Main bearings ....Five
Main bearing diameter 1.875in
Bearing width, front to rear...........2.0, 1.0, 1.625, 1.0, 2.0in
Bearing clearance........................0.0025in
Cylinder head...............................Integral, cast iron
Compression ratio.......................About 9.0:1
Cylinder block..............................Four cylinders each block, 7.25in high
Crankcase type & material...........Barrel, aluminum
Main-bearing supports.................Bronze diaphragms, spigoted into case
Lubrication system.......................Dry sump, two gear pumps
Oil capacity ....4.5 gal
Carburetor....................................One Winfield 2in Type SR
Supercharger................................Miller centrifugal
Supercharger drive ratio...............About 5:1
Supercharge pressure ....Client's preference
Supercharger intercooler..............Client's preference
Supercharger impeller diam. 6–8in

Exhaust system ....Eight-branch manifold; collector pipe optional
Water pump...................................Centrifugal
Cooling system capacity ....4 gal
Ignition system.............................Robert Bosch magneto, Type FHa8
Spark plugs..................................One per cyl.; Champion J10
Spark advance.............................Manual
Spark-advance crankshaft degrees ......33 degrees
Horsepower..................................230 at 8,000rpm; often higher
Flywheel diameter 9.5in
Clutch type...................................9in, four-face, self-locking, except rear drive
Transmission................................Three spur gears and reverse
Engine mounts ....Three
Transmission mounts...................Three
Engine weight...............................290lb, exclusive of magneto

Chassis

Frame...0.125in mild steel in 5in channels
Wheelbase....................................100in
Tread
      front 52in
      rear 52in
Suspension
      rear-drive............................Half-elliptic springs
      front-drive ....Double quarter-elliptic front, half elliptic rear
Shock absorbers ....Hartford type
Wheel-spindle type ....Ball bearing
Steering turns, lock to lock............1.4
Brake type ....Mechanical servo
Brake friction area ....To 285sq-in
Hubs
      rear-drive............................Rudge 52mm
      front-drive ....Rudge 62mm front, 32mm rear
Wheels...20in triple-laced wire lock-ring type
Tire size..525x20in
Tire inflation pressure 30–35psi
Fuel capacity ....About 34 gal
Body material ....Aluminum sheet
Vehicle dry weight........................About 1,400lb
Instruments ....Supercharger pressure, tachometer, water temperature, air pressure, fuel-tank pressure

Appendix III: Harry Miller's US Patents

Researched and compiled by Michael D. Rosen

Miller was noted for the abundance of his innovative ideas—and for the fact that he rarely took the trouble to try to patent any of them. For instance, patent 1,649,361, for what was generally termed "the front-drive unit," was unknown even to Leo Goossen when Robert Fabris of the Auburn-Cord-Duesenberg Club brought it to the author's attention in 1964.

813,104. Sparking device. Filed January 14, 1905, issued February 20, 1906.

872,075. Sparking device. Miller and Benjamin G. Gilbough. Filed February 14, 1906, issued November 26, 1907.

872,629. Sparking device. Miller and Benjamin G. Gilbough. Filed February 14, 1906, issued December 3, 1907.

876,472. Internal-combustion engine. Miller and Frank M. Adamson c/o 40/100 Frank P. Harris, 40/100 A. T. Hay, 20/100 H. A. Miller. Filed September 4, 1906, issued January 14, 1908.

943,197. Carburetor. c/o Miller Carburetor & Mfg. Co. Filed January 11, 1909, issued December 14, 1909.

962,649. Carburetor. Filed November 16, 1909, issued June 28, 1910.

983,247. Carburetor. Filed March 3, 1910, issued January 31, 1911.

995,623. Carburetor. Filed November 16, 1909, issued June 20, 1911.

1,036,301. Carburetor. Filed October 19, 1910, issued August 20, 1912.

1,036,302. Auxiliary air attachment. Filed November 14, 1910, issued August 20, 1912.

1,065,462. Carburetor. c/o New-Miller Mfg. Co. Filed June 7, 1911, issued June 24, 1913.

1,094,674. Carburetor. Miller and Frank M. Adamson. Filed September 12, 1912, issued April 28, 1914.

1,183,221. Double-fuel carburetor. Miller and Frank M. Adamson c/o Master Carburetor Co. Filed May 4, 1914, issued May 16, 1916.

1,183,222. Carburetor. c/o Master Carburetor Co. Filed May 20, 1914, issued May 16, 1916.

1,014,319. Carburetor attachment. Filed April 18, 1910, issued January 9, 1912.

1,213,807. Carburetor. Miller and Clarence J. Cadwell c/o Master Carburetor Co. Filed May 4, 1914, issued January 23, 1917.

NA. Carburetor. Miller and Frank M. Adamson c/o Master Carburetor Co. Filed May 1, 1916, issued May 29, 1917.

1,231,773. Carburetor. Miller and Frank M. Adamson c/o Master Carburetor Co. Filed February 10, 1914, issued July 3, 1917.

1,236,096. Carburetor. Miller and Frank M. Adamson c/o Master Carburetor Co. Filed April 26, 1916, issued August 7, 1917.

1,272,695. Carburetor. Miller and Frank M. Adamson. Filed September 18, 1916, issued July 16, 1918.

1,301,483. Carburetor. Miller and Frank M. Adamson. Filed May 1, 1916, issued April 22, 1919.

Design Patent 55,070. Automobile. Filed September 22, 1919, issued May 4, 1920.

1,649,361. Drive mechanism for vehicles. Filed January 30, 1925, issued November 15, 1927.

1,828,327. Issued October 20, 1931.

2,080,291. Clutch. Miller, c/o H. A. Miller Engineering Corp. Filed April 6, 1935, issued May 11, 1937.

2,095,393. Transmission. Miller, c/o H. A. Miller Engineering Corp. Filed March 12, 1935, issued October 12, 1937.

2,114,452. Wheel mounting. Miller, c/o H. A. Miller Engineering Corp. Filed April 26, 1935, issued April 19, 1938. (Independent suspension).

Design Patent 106,275. Airplane. Frank M. Bellanca. Filed June 9, 1937, issued October 5, 1937.

Airplane Construction Patent

2,140,783. Frank M. Bellanca c/o Miller-Bellanca Airplanes, Ltd. Filed August 3, 1937, issued December 20, 1938.

Appendix IV: Miller and Offenhauser Championship Car Winners

NOTES: * = *National Championship event*, B = *Board Track*, P = *Paved Track*, D = *Dirt Track*, s = *supercharged engine*, t = *turbocharged engine*, m = *marine engine*.

Compiled by James O'Keefe and Joseph Freeman from their work in progress, Encyclopedia of Auto Racing Winners.

Numerous sources and the input of many have helped with the compilation of this listing, but thanks and grateful acknowledgements must especially be given to Ken McMahen. John Printz, Phil Harms, Bill Digney, Bruce Craig, John Kozub and Dick Goodfellows also made significant contributions.

Date	Track	Miles	Winner	Chassis	Engine	Cyl.	CID
09-03-17	Uniontown	113 B	Frank Elliott	Delage	Miller	4	289
10-13-17	Chicago	20 B	Tom Alley	Miller	Miller	4	289
07-19-19	Uniontown	23 B	Roscoe Sarles	Miller	Miller	4	289
07-04-21	Tacoma	242* B	Tommy Milton	Miller	Miller	8	181
03-05-22	Beverly Hills	250* B	Tommy Milton	Miller	Miller	8	181
04-02-22	Beverly Hills	25* B	Tommy Milton	Miller	Miller	8	181
04-02-22	Beverly Hills	25* B	Frank Elliott	Miller	Miller	8	181
04-02-22	Beverly Hills	50* B	Tommy Milton	Miller	Miller	8	181
05-07-22	Cotati	100* B	Jimmy Murphy	Duesenberg	Miller	8	181
05-30-22	Indianapolis	500* P	Jimmy Murphy	Duesenberg	Miller	8	181
06-17-22	Uniontown	225* B	Jimmy Murphy	Duesenberg	Miller	8	181
07-04-22	Tacoma	242* B	Jimmy Murphy	Duesenberg	Miller	8	181
08-06-22	Cotati	50* B	Frank Elliott	Miller	Miller	8	181
08-06-22	Cotati	100* B	Frank Elliott	Miller	Miller	8	181
09-17-22	Kansas City	300* B	Tommy Milton	Miller	Miller	8	181
09-30-22	Fresno	150* B	Bennett Hill	Miller	Miller	8	181
10-29-22	Cotati	100 B	Bennett Hill	Miller	Miller	8	181
12-03-22	Beverly Hills	250* B	Jimmy Murphy	Miller	Miller	8	181
02-25-23	Beverly Hills	250* B	Jimmy Murphy	Miller	Miller	8	181
04-26-23	Fresno	150* B	Jimmy Murphy	Miller	Miller	8	121
05-30-23	Indianapolis	500* P	Tommy Milton	Miller	Miller	8	121
07-04-23	Kansas City	250* B	Eddie Hearne	Miller	Miller	8	121
09-04-23	Altoona	200* B	Eddie Hearne	Miller	Miller	8	121
09-15-23	Syracuse	100 D	Tommy Milton	Miller	Miller	8	121
09-29-23	Fresno	150* B	Harry Hartz	Miller	Miller	8	121
10-21-23	Kansas City	250* B	Harlan Fengler	Miller	Miller	8	121
11-29-23	Beverly Hills	250* B	Bennett Hill	Miller	Miller	8	121
02-24-24	Beverly Hills	250* B	Harlan Fengler	Miller	Miller	8	121
06-14-24	Altoona	250* B	Jimmy Murphy	Miller	Miller	8	121
07-04-24	Kansas City	150* B	Jimmy Murphy	Miller	Miller	8	121
09-01-24	Altoona	250* B	Jimmy Murphy	Miller	Miller	8	121
10-02-24	Fresno	150* B	Earl Cooper	Miller	Miller	8	121
10-25-24	Charlotte	250* B	Tommy Milton	Miller	Miller	8	121
11-16-24	Tanforan	100 D	Ralph DePalma	Miller	Miller	8	121s
12-14-24	Culver City	250* B	Bennett Hill	Miller	Miller	8	121s
03-01-25	Culver City	250* B	Tommy Milton	Miller	Miller	8	121s
04-11-25	Dallas	100 D	Ralph DePalma	Miller	Miller	8	121s
04-19-25	Culver City	25 B	Leon Duray	Miller	Miller	8	121s
04-19-25	Culver City	25 B	Bob McDonough	Miller	Miller	8	121s
04-19-25	Culver City	50 B	Harry Hartz	Miller	Miller	8	121s
05-11-25	Charlotte	250* B	Earl Cooper	Miller	Miller	8	121s
07-04-25	Rockingham	100 D	Ralph DePalma	Miller	Miller	8	121s
07-18-25	Denver	100 D	Ralph DePalma	Miller	Miller	8	121s
09-07-25	Altoona	250* B	Bob McDonough	Miller	Miller	8	121s
09-19-25	Syracuse	100 D	Ralph DePalma	Miller	Miller	8	121s
10-03-25	Fresno	150 B	Fred Comer	Miller	Miller	8	121s
10-26-25	Laurel	250* B	Bob McDonough	Miller	Miller	8	121s
11-29-25	Culver City	250* B	Frank Elliott	Miller	Miller	8	121s
03-21-26	Culver City	250* B	Bennett Hill	Miller	Miller	8	121s
05-01-26	Atlantic City	300* B	Harry Hartz	Miller	Miller	8	121s
05-10-26	Charlotte	250* B	Earl DeVore	Miller	Miller	8	121s
05-31-26	Indianapolis	400* P	Frank Lockhart	Miller	Miller	8	90s
06-12-26	Altoona	250* B	Dave Lewis	Miller FD	Miller	8	90s
06-19-26	Laurel	99 B	Jimmy Gleason	Miller	Miller	8	181
06-27-26	Detroit	100 D	Frank Lockhart	Miller	Miller	8	181
07-05-26	Rockingham	200* B	Earl Cooper	Miller FD	Miller	8	90s
07-17-26	Atlantic City	60* B	Harry Hartz	Miller	Miller	8	90s
07-17-26	Atlantic City	60* B	Norman Batten	Miller	Miller	8	91s
07-17-26	Atlantic City	60* B	Fred Comer	Miller	Miller	8	90s
07-17-26	Atlantic City	120* B	Harry Hartz	Miller	Miller	8	90s
08-15-26	Kalamazoo	100 D	Phil Shafer	Miller	Miller	8	90s
08-23-26	Charlotte	25* B	Earl Cooper	Miller FD	Miller	8	90s
08-23-26	Charlotte	25* B	Dave Lewis	Miller FD	Miller	8	90s
08-23-26	Charlotte	50* B	Frank Lockhart	Miller	Miller	8	90s
08-23-26	Charlotte	150* B	Frank Lockhart	Miller	Miller	8	90s
09-11-26	Detroit	100 D	Frank Lockhart	Miller	Miller	8	90s
09-18-26	Altoona	250* B	Frank Lockhart	Miller	Miller	8	90s
09-25-26	Laurel	99 B	Jimmy Gleason	Miller	Miller	8	181
10-02-26	Fresno	50 B	Frank Lockhart	Miller	Miller	8	90s
10-09-26	Langhorne	100 D	Russ Snowberger	Miller	Miller	8	181
10-12-26	Rockingham	25* B	Bennett Hill	Miller	Miller	8	90s
10-12-26	Rockingham	25* B	Leon Duray	Miller FD	Miller	8	90s
10-12-26	Rockingham	200* B	Harry Hartz	Miller	Miller	8	90s

Date	Track	Miles	Winner	Chassis	Engine	Cyl.	CID
11-11-26	Charlotte	25* B	Frank Lockhart	Miller	Miller	8	90s
11-11-26	Charlotte	25* B	Dave Lewis	Miller FD	Miller	8	90s
11-11-26	Charlotte	50* B	Harry Hartz	Miller	Miller	8	90s
11-11-26	Charlotte	100* B	Leon Duray	Miller FD	Miller	8	90s
03-26-27	Culver City	250* B	Leon Duray	Miller FD	Miller	8	90s
05-07-27	Atlantic City	201 B	Dave Lewis	Miller FD	Miller	8	90s
06-05-27	Detroit	100 D	Frank Lockhart	Miller	Miller	8	90s
06-11-27	Altoona	200* B	Peter DePaolo	Miller FD	Miller	8	90s
06-19-27	Kalamazoo	100 D	Fred Frame	Miller	Miller	8	121s
07-04-27	Rockingham	200* B	Peter DePaolo	Miller FD	Miller	8	90s
07-31-27	Detroit	100 D	Cliff Woodbury	Miller	Miller	8	90s
08-14-27	Kalamazoo	100 D	Frank Lockhart	Miller	Miller	8	90s
08-21-27	Toledo	100 D	Frank Lockhart	Miller	Miller	8	90s
09-03-27	Syracuse	100 D	Frank Lockhart	Miller	Miller	8	90s
09-05-27	Altoona	200* B	Frank Lockhart	Miller	Miller	8	90s
09-10-27	Langhorne	100 D	Ray Keech	Miller	Miller	8	121s
09-19-27	Charlotte	25* B	Frank Lockhart	Miller	Miller	8	90s
09-19-27	Charlotte	50*	Peter De Paolo	Miller FD	Miller	8	90s
09-19-27	Charlotte	100* B	Babe Stapp	Miller	Miller	8	90s
09-25-27	Cleveland	100 D	Frank Lockhart	Miller	Miller	8	90s
10-02-27	Milwaukee	56 D	Lou Schneider	Miller	Miller	8	91s
10-12-27	Rockingham	65* B	Frank Lockhart	Miller	Miller	8	90s
10-12-27	Rockingham	75* B	Frank Lockhart	Miller	Miller	8	90s
10-16-27	Detroit	50 D	Cliff Woodbury	Miller	Miller	8	90s
10-16-27	Detroit	50 D	Cliff Woodbury	Miller	Miller	8	90s
05-27-28	Toledo	100 D	Chet Gardner	Miller	Miller	8	121s
05-30-28	Indianapolis	500* P	Lou Meyer	Miller	Miller	8	90s
06-10-28	Detroit	100* D	Ray Keech	Miller	Miller	8	90s
07-04-28	Rockingham	15* B	Leon Duray	Miller FD	Miller	8	90s
07-04-28	Rockingham	185* B	Ray Keech	Miller	Miller	8	90s
07-15-28	Detroit	100 D	Howard Taylor	Miller FD	Miller	8	91s
08-12-28	Kalamazoo	100 D	Chet Gardner	Miller	Miller	8	121s
08-19-28	Altoona	200* B	Lou Meyer	Miller	Miller	8	90s
09-01-28	Syracuse	100* D	Ray Keech	Miller	Miller	8	90s
09-09-28	Akron	100 B	Cliff Woodbury	Miller FD	Miller	8	90s
09-16-28	Atlantic City	101 B	Ray Keech	Miller	Miller	8	90s
10-12-28	Rockingham	63* B	Cliff Woodbury	Miller FD	Miller	8	90s
05-26-29	Toledo	100 D	Wilbur Shaw	Miller	Miller	4m	150s
05-30-29	Indianapolis	500* P	Ray Keech	Miller	Miller	8	90s
05-30-29	Bridgeville	100 B	Wilbur Shaw	Miller	Miller	4m	150s
06-02-29	Cleveland	85 D	Wilbur Shaw	Miller	Miller	4m	150s
06-09-29	Detroit	100* D	Cliff Woodbury	Miller	Miller	8	90s
06-15-29	Altoona	149* B	Lou Meyer	Miller	Miller	8	90s
06-30-29	Woodbridge	100 B	Lou Moore	Miller	Miller	8	90s
07-04-29	Bridgeville	100 B	Wilbur Shaw	Miller	Miller	4m	150s
08-04-29	Woodbridge	100 B	Lou Moore	Miller	Miller	8	90s
08-18-29	Toledo	100 D	Wilbur Shaw	Miller	Miller	4m	150s
08-31-29	Syracuse	100* D	Wilbur Shaw	Miller	Miller	4m	150s
09-02-29	Altoona	200* B	Lou Meyer	Miller	Miller	8	90s
09-22-29	Cleveland	100 D	Deacon Litz	Miller	Miller	8	90s
10-06-29	Ashland	100 D	Wilbur Shaw	Miller	Miller	4m	150s
05-03-30	Langhorne	100* D	Bill Cummings	Miller	Miller	8	90s
05-25-30	Toledo	100 D	Bill Albertson	Miller	Miller	8	91s
05-30-30	Indianapolis	500* P	Billy Arnold	Sommers FD	Miller	8	151
06-09-30	Detroit	100* D	Wilbur Shaw	Dreyer	Miller	4m	150
06-14-30	Altoona	200* B	Billy Arnold	Sommers FD	Miller	8	151
06-22-30	Akron	100* B	Shorty Cantlon	Miller	Miller	4m	182
07-04-30	Bridgeville	100* B	Wilbur Shaw	Miller	Miller	4m	150
07-04-30	Langhorne	100 D	Fred Frame	Miller	Miller	8	90s
09-01-30	Altoona	116* B	Billy Arnold	Sommers FD	Miller	8	151
09-14-30	Toledo	100 D	Frank Brisko	Miller	Miller	8	151
09-28-30	Akron	81 B	Wilbur Shaw	Miller	Miller	8	90
10-18-30	Langhorne	100 D	Frank Farmer	Miller	Miller	8	101s
05-30-31	Indianapolis	500* P	Lou Schneider	Stevens	Miller	8	151
06-14-31	Detroit	100* D	Lou Meyer	Stevens	Miller	8	230
06-21-31	Roby	100 D	Lou Schneider	Stevens	Miller	8	151
07-04-31	Altoona	100* B	Lou Moore	Miller	Miller	8	230
09-07-31	Altoona	25* B	Shorty Cantlon	Stevens	Miller	8	151
09-07-31	Altoona	100* B	Shorty Cantlon	Stevens	Miller	8	151
09-12-31	Syracuse	100* D	Lou Moore	Miller	Miller	8	230
05-30-32	Indianapolis	500* P	Fred Frame	Wetteroth FD	Miller	8	182
06-05-32	Detroit	83* D	Bob Carey	Stevens	Miller	8	249
06-19-32	Roby	100* D	S. Stubblefield	Adams	Miller	4	220
07-02-32	Syracuse	81* D	Bob Carey	Stevens	Miller	8	249
09-10-32	Detroit	100* D	Mauri Rose	Stevens	Miller	8	220
11-13-32	Oakland	150* D	Bill Cummings	Miller	Miller	8	268
05-30-33	Indianapolis	500* P	Lou Meyer	Miller	Miller	8	258
06-11-33	Detroit	100* D	Bill Cummings	Miller	Miller	8	268
09-09-33	Syracuse	100* D	Bill Cummings	Miller	Miller	8	268
05-30-34	Indianapolis	500* P	Bill Cummings	Rigling FD	Miller	4	220
08-25-34	Springfield	100* D	Billy Winn	Stevens	Miller	4	220
09-09-34	Syracuse	100* D	Shorty Cantlon	Weil	Miller	4	220

Date	Track	Miles	Winner	Chassis	Engine	Cyl.	CID
12-23-34	Mines Field	197* R	Kelly Petillo	Sommers	Sparks	4	269
05-30-35	Indianapolis	500* P	Kelly Petillo	Wetteroth	Offy	4	262
07-04-35	St. Paul	100* D	Kelly Petillo	Wetteroth	Offy	4	262
08-24-35	Springfield	100* D	Billy Winn	Duesenberg	Miller	4	255
09-02-35	Syracuse	100* D	Billy Winn	Duesenberg	Miller	4	255
09-07-35	Altoona	100* D	Lou Meyer	Stevens	Miller	4	255
10-13-35	Langhorne	100* D	Kelly Petillo	Wetteroth	Offy	4	262
12-15-35	Ascot	125 D	Rex Mays	Sommers	Sparks	4	203
01-12-36	Oakland	150 D	Al Gordon	Weil	Miller	4	228
01-26-36	Ascot	125 D	Rex Mays	Sommers	Sparks	4	203
05-30-36	Indianapolis	500* P	Lou Meyer	Stevens	Miller	4	255
06-20-36	Goshen	100* D	Rex Mays	Sommers	Sparks	4	239
09-15-36	Syracuse	100* D	Mauri Rose	Stevens	Offy	4	270
05-31-37	Indianapolis	500* P	Wilbur Shaw	Stevens	Offy	4	255
09-12-37	Syracuse	100* D	Billy Winn	Weil	Miller	4	255
05-30-38	Indianapolis	500* P	Floyd Roberts	Wetteroth	Offy	4	270
09-10-38	Syracuse	100* D	Jimmy Snyder	Dreyer	Offy	4	255
08-27-39	Milwaukee	100* D	Babe Stapp	Stevens	Offy	4	255
09-02-39	Syracuse	100* D	Mauri Rose	Wetteroth	Offy	4	270
08-24-40	Springfield	100* D	Rex Mays	Stevens	Winfield	8	180s
09-02-40	Syracuse	100* D	Rex Mays	Stevens	Winfield	8	180s
05-30-41	Indianapolis	500* P	Floyd Davis/Mauri Rose	Wetteroth	Offy	4	270
08-24-41	Milwaukee	100* D	Rex Mays	Stevens	Winfield	8	180s
09-01-41	Syracuse	100* D	Rex Mays	Stevens	Winfield	8	180s
05-30-46	Indianapolis	500* P	George Robson	Adams	Sparks	6	183s
06-30-46	Langhorne	100* D	Rex Mays	Stevens	Winfield	8	180s
09-02-46	Atlanta	98* D	George Connor	Kurtis	Offy	4	270
09-15-46	Indianapolis	100* D	Rex Mays	Stevens	Winfield	8	180s
09-22-46	Milwaukee	100* D	Rex Mays	Stevens	Winfield	8	180s
10-06-46	Goshen	100* D	Tony Bettenhausen	Wetteroth	Offy	4	270
05-30-47	Indianapolis	500* P	Mauri Rose	Diedt FD	Offy	4	270
06-08-47	Milwaukee	100* D	Bill Holland	Wetteroth	Offy	4	270
06-22-47	Langhorne	100* D	Bill Holland	Wetteroth	Offy	4	270
07-04-47	Atlanta	77* D	Walt Ader	Adams	Sparks	4	203
07-13-47	Bainbridge	90* D	Ted Horn	Blake	Offy	4	233
07-27-47	Milwaukee	100* D	Charles van Acker	Stevens	Offy	4	255
08-17-47	Goshen	100* D	Tony Bettenhausen	Stevens	Offy	4	255
08-24-47	Milwaukee	100* D	Ted Horn	Blake	Offy	4	233
09-28-47	Springfield	100* D	Tony Bettenhausen	Stevens	Offy	4	255
11-02-47	Arlington	101* D	Ted Horn	Blake	Offy	4	233
04-25-48	Arlington	101* D	Ted Horn	Blake	Offy	4	233
05-31-48	Indianapolis	500* P	Mauri Rose	Diedt FD	Offy	4	270
06-06-48	Milwaukee	100* D	Emil Andres	Kurtis	Offy	4	270
06-20-48	Langhorne	100* D	Walt Brown	Kurtis	Offy	4	270
08-15-48	Milwaukee	100* D	Johnny Mantz	Kurtis	Offy	4	270
08-21-48	Springfield	100* D	Ted Horn	Blake	Offy	4	233
08-29-48	Milwaukee	200* D	Myron Fohr/Tony Bettenhausen	Marchese	Offy	4	270
09-04-48	DuQuoin	100* D	Lee Wallard	Meyer	Offy	4	233
09-06-48	Atlanta	100* D	Mel Hansen	Wetteroth	Offy	4	270
09-19-48	Springfield	100* D	Myron Fohr	Marchese	Offy	4	270
10-10-48	DuQuoin	100* D	Johnnie Parsons	Kurtis	Offy	4	270
04-24-49	Arlington	101* D	Johnnie Parsons	Kurtis	Offy	4	270
05-30-49	Indianapolis	500* P	Bill Holland	Diedt FD	Offy	4	270
06-05-49	Milwaukee	100* D	Myron Fohr	Marchese	Offy	4	270
06-19-49	Trenton	100* D	Myron Fohr	Marchese	Offy	4	270
08-20-49	Springfield	100* D	Mel Hansen	Lesovsky	Offy	4	270
08-28-49	Milwaukee	200* D	Johnnie Parsons	Kurtis	Offy	4	270
09-03-49	DuQuoin	100* D	Tony Bettenhausen	Kurtis	Offy	4	107s
09-10-49	Syracuse	100* D	Johnnie Parsons	Kurtis	Offy	4	270
09-11-49	Detroit	100* D	Tony Bettenhausen	Kurtis	Offy	4	107s
09-25-49	Springfield	100* D	Johnnie Parsons	Kurtis	Offy	4	270
10-16-49	Langhorne	100* D	Johnnie Parsons	Kurtis	Offy	4	270
10-30-49	Sacramento	100* D	Fred Agabashian	Kurtis	Offy	4	270
11-06-49	Del Mar	100* D	Jimmy Davies	Ewing	Offy	4	270
05-30-50	Indianapolis	500* P	Johnnie Parsons	Kurtis	Offy	4	270
06-11-50	Milwaukee	100* D	Tony Bettenhausen	Wetteroth	Offy	4	270
06-25-50	Langhorne	100* D	Jack McGrath	Kurtis	Offy	4	270
08-19-50	Springfield	100* D	Paul Russo	Silnes	Offy	4	270
08-27-50	Milwaukee	200* D	Walt Faulkner	Kurtis	Offy	4	270
09-09-50	Syracuse	100* D	Jack McGrath	Kurtis	Offy	4	270
09-10-50	Detroit	100* D	Henry Banks	Moore	Offy	4	270
10-01-50	Springfield	100* D	Tony Bettenhausen	Kurtis	Offy	4	107s
10-15-50	Sacramento	100* D	Duke Dismore	Kurtis	Offy	4	270
11-12-50	Phoenix	100* D	Jimmy Davies	Ewing	Offy	4	270
11-26-50	Bay Meadows	149* D	Tony Bettenhausen	Kurtis	Offy	4	107s
12-10-50	Darlington	200* P	Johnnie Parsons	Silnes	Offy	4	270

Date	Track	Miles	Winner	Chassis	Engine	Cyl.	CID
05-30-51	Indianapolis	500* P	Lee Wallard	Kurtis	Offy	4	241
06-10-51	Milwaukee	100* D	Tony Bettenhausen	Kurtis	Offy	4	241
06-24-51	Langhorne	100* D	Tony Bettenhausen	Kurtis	Offy	4	241
07-04-51	Darlington	250* P	Walt Faulkner	Kuzma	Offy	4	270
08-18-51	Springfield	100* D	Tony Bettenhausen	Kurtis	Offy	4	241
08-26-51	Milwaukee	200* D	Walt Faulkner	Kuzma	Offy	4	270
09-01-51	DuQuoin	100* D	Tony Bettenhausen	Kurtis	Offy	4	241
09-03-51	DuQuoin	101* D	Tony Bettenhausen	Kurtis	Offy	4	241
09-08-51	Syracuse	67* D	Tony Bettenhausen	Kurtis	Offy	4	241
09-09-51	Detroit	100* D	Paul Russo	Silnes	Offy	4	270
09-23-51	Denver	100* D	Tony Bettenhausen	Kurtis	Offy	4	241
10-21-51	San Jose	100* D	Tony Bettenhausen	Kurtis	Offy	4	241
11-04-51	Phoenix	100* D	Johnnie Parsons	Kurtis	Offy	4	270
11-11-51	Bay Meadows	150* D	Johnnie Parsons	Kurtis	Offy	4	270
05-30-52	Indianapolis	500* P	Troy Ruttman	Kuzma	Offy	4	263
06-08-52	Milwaukee	100* D	Mike Nazaruk	Kurtis	Offy	4	263
07-04-52	Raleigh	200* P	Troy Ruttman	Kuzma	Offy	4	263
08-16-52	Springfield	100* D	Bill Schindler	Silnes	Offy	4	270
08-24-52	Milwaukee	200* D	Chuck Stevenson	Kurtis	Offy	4	263
08-30-52	Detroit	100* D	Bill Vukovich	Kuzma	Offy	4	263
09-01-52	DuQuoin	100* D	Chuck Stevenson	Kurtis	Offy	4	263
09-06-52	Syracuse	100* D	Jack McGrath	Kurtis	Offy	4	270
09-28-52	Denver	100* D	Bill Vukovich	Kuzma	Offy	4	263
11-02-52	San Jose	100* D	Bobby Ball	Kurtis	Offy	4	270
11-11-52	Phoenix	100* D	Johnnie Parsons	Kurtis	Offy	4	270
05-30-53	Indianapolis	500* P	Bill Vukovich	Kurtis	Offy	4	270
06-07-53	Milwaukee	100* D	Jack McGrath	Kurtis	Offy	4	270
06-21-53	Springfield	100* D	Rodger Ward	Kurtis	Offy	4	270
07-04-53	Detroit	51* D	Rodger Ward	Kurtis	Offy	4	270
08-22-53	Springfield	100* D	Sam Hanks	Kurtis	Offy	4	270
08-30-53	Milwaukee	200* D	Chuck Stevenson	Kuzma	Offy	4	263
09-07-53	DuQuoin	100* D	Sam Hanks	Kurtis	Offy	4	270
09-12-53	Syracuse	100* D	Tony Bettenhausen	Kurtis	Offy	4	270
09-26-53	Indianapolis	100* D	Bob Sweikert	Kuzma	Offy	4	270
10-25-53	Sacramento	100* D	Jimmy Bryan	Kurtis	Offy	4	263
11-11-53	Phoenix	100* D	Tony Bettenhausen	Kurtis	Offy	4	270
05-31-54	Indianapolis	500* P	Bill Vukovich	Kurtis	Offy	4	270
06-06-54	Milwaukee	100* P	Chuck Stevenson	Kuzma	Offy	4	270
06-20-54	Langhorne	100* P	Jimmy Bryan	Kuzma	Offy	4	270
07-05-54	Darlington	201* P	Manny Ayulo	Kuzma	Offy	4	270
08-21-54	Springfield	100* D	Jimmy Davies	Ewing	Offy	4	270
08-29-54	Milwaukee	200* P	Manny Ayulo	Kuzma	Offy	4	270
09-06-54	DuQuoin	83* D	Sam Hanks	Kurtis	Offy	4	270
09-11-54	Syracuse	100* D	Bob Sweikert	Kurtis	Offy	4	270
09-18-54	Indianapolis	100* D	Jimmy Bryan	Kuzma	Offy	4	270
10-17-54	Sacramento	100* D	Jimmy Bryan	Kuzma	Offy	4	270
11-08-54	Phoenix	100* D	Jimmy Bryan	Kuzma	Offy	4	270
11-14-54	Las Vegas	100* D	Jimmy Bryan	Kuzma	Offy	4	270
05-30-55	Indianapolis	500* P	Bob Sweikert	Kurtis	Offy	4	270
06-05-55	Milwaukee	100* P	Johnny Thomson	Kuzma	Offy	4	270
06-26-55	Langhorne	100* D	Jimmy Bryan	Kuzma	Offy	4	270
08-20-55	Springfield	100* D	Jimmy Bryan	Kuzma	Offy	4	270
08-28-55	Milwaukee	250* P	Pat Flaherty	Kurtis	Offy	4	270
09-05-55	DuQuoin	100* D	Jimmy Bryan	Kuzma	Offy	4	270
09-10-55	Syracuse	100* D	Bob Sweikert	Watson	Offy	4	270
09-17-55	Indianapolis	100* D	Jimmy Bryan	Kuzma	Offy	4	270
10-16-55	Sacramento	100* D	Jimmy Bryan	Kuzma	Offy	4	270
11-06-55	Phoenix	97* D	Jimmy Bryan	Kuzma	Offy	4	270
05-30-56	Indianapolis	500* P	Pat Flaherty	Watson	Offy	4	270
06-10-56	Milwaukee	100* P	Pat Flaherty	Watson	Offy	4	270
06-24-56	Langhorne	100* D	George Amick	Kuzma	Offy	4	270
07-04-56	Darlington	201* P	Pat O'Connor	Templeton	Offy	4	270
07-14-56	Atlanta	100* D	Eddie Sachs	Scopa	Offy	4	270
08-18-56	Springfield	100* D	Jimmy Bryan	Kuzma	Offy	4	270
08-26-56	Milwaukee	250* P	Jimmy Bryan	Kuzma	Offy	4	270
09-03-56	DuQuoin	100* D	Jimmy Bryan	Kuzma	Offy	4	270
09-08-56	Syracuse	100* D	Tony Bettenhausen	Kuzma	Offy	4	270
09-15-56	Indianapolis	100* D	Jimmy Bryan	Kuzma	Offy	4	270
10-21-56	Sacramento	100* D	Jud Larson	Watson	Offy	4	270
11-12-56	Phoenix	100* D	George Amick	Lesovsky	Offy	4	270
05-30-57	Indianapolis	500* P	Sam Hanks	Epperly	Offy	4	250
06-02-57	Langhorne	100* D	Johnny Thomson	Kuzma	Offy	4	252
06-09-57	Milwaukee	100* D	Rodger Ward	Lesovsky	Offy	4	166s
06-23-57	Detroit	100* D	Jimmy Bryan	Kuzma	Offy	4	252
06-29-57	Monza	499 P	Jimmy Bryan	Kuzma	Offy	4	252
07-04-57	Atlanta	100* D	George Amick	Lesovsky	Offy	4	255
08-17-57	Springfield	100* D	Rodger Ward	Lesovsky	Offy	4	252
08-25-57	Milwaukee	200* D	Jim Rathmann	Epperly	Offy	4	255
09-02-57	DuQuoin	100* D	Jud Larson	Watson	Offy	4	252
09-07-57	Syracuse	100* D	Elmer George	Watson	Offy	4	252
09-14-57	Indianapolis	100* P	Jud Larson	Watson	Offy	4	252
09-29-57	Trenton	100* P	Pat O'Connor	Kuzma	Offy	4	255
10-20-57	Sacramento	100* D	Rodger Ward	Lesovsky	Offy	4	252

Date	Track	Miles	Winner	Chassis	Engine	Cyl.	CID
11-11-57	Phoenix	100* D	Jimmy Bryan	Kuzma	Offy	4	252
03-30-58	Trenton	100* P	Len Sutton	Kuzma	Offy	4	252
05-30-58	Indianapolis	500* P	Jimmy Bryan	Epperly	Offy	4	252
06-08-58	Milwaukee	100* P	Art Bisch	Kuzma	Offy	4	252
06-15-58	Langhorne	100* D	Eddie Sachs	Kuzma	Offy	4	255
06-29-58	Monza	499 P	Jim Rathmann	Watson	Offy	4	252
07-04-58	Atlanta	100* D	Jud Larson	Watson	Offy	4	252
08-16-58	Springfield	100* D	Johnny Thomson	Kuzma	Offy	4	252
08-24-58	Milwaukee	200* P	Rodger Ward	Lesovsky	Offy	4	252
09-01-58	DuQuoin	100* D	Johnny Thomson	Kuzma	Offy	4	252
09-06-58	Syracuse	100* D	Johnny Thomson	Kuzma	Offy	4	252
09-13-58	Indianapolis	100* D	Eddie Sachs	Kuzma	Offy	4	255
09-28-58	Trenton	100* P	Rodger Ward	Lesovsky	Offy	4	252
10-26-58	Sacramento	100* D	Johnny Thomson	Kuzma	Offy	4	252
11-11-58	Phoenix	100* D	Jud Larson	Lesovsky	Offy	4	252
04-04-59	Daytona	100* P	Jim Rathmann	Watson	Offy	4	252
04-19-59	Trenton	87* P	Tony Bettenhausen	Kuzma	Offy	4	252
05-30-59	Indianapolis	500* P	Rodger Ward	Watson	Offy	4	252
06-07-59	Milwaukee	100* P	Johnny Thomson	Lesovsky	Offy	4	252
06-14-59	Langhorne	100* D	Van Johnson	Kurtis	Offy	4	252
08-22-59	Springfield	100* D	Len Sutton	Kuzma	Offy	4	252
08-30-59	Milwaukee	200* P	Rodger Ward	Watson	Offy	4	252
09-07-59	DuQuoin	100* D	Rodger Ward	Watson	Offy	4	252
09-12-59	Syracuse	100* D	Eddie Sachs	Meskowski	Offy	4	252
09-19-59	Indianapolis	100* P	Rodger Ward	Watson	Offy	4	252
09-27-59	Trenton	100* P	Eddie Sachs	Meskowski	Offy	4	252
10-18-59	Phoenix	100* D	Tony Bettenhausen	Kuzma	Offy	4	252
10-25-59	Sacramento	100* D	Jim Hurtubise	Kuzma	Offy	4	252
04-10-60	Trenton	100* P	Rodger Ward	Watson	Offy	4	252
05-30-60	Indianapolis	500* P	Jim Rathmann	Watson	Offy	4	252
06-05-60	Milwaukee	100* P	Rodger Ward	Watson	Offy	4	252
06-19-60	Langhorne	100* D	Jim Hurtubise	Kuzma	Offy	4	252
08-20-60	Springfield	100* D	Jim Packard	Lesovsky	Offy	4	252
08-28-60	Milwaukee	200* P	Len Sutton	Watson	Offy	4	252
09-05-60	DuQuoin	100* D	A.J. Foyt Jr.	Meskowski	Offy	4	252
09-10-60	Syracuse	100* D	Bobby Grim	Meskowski	Offy	4	252
09-17-60	Indianapolis	100* D	A.J. Foyt Jr.	Meskowski	Offy	4	252
09-25-60	Trenton	100* P	Eddie Sachs	Kuzma	Offy	4	252
10-30-60	Sacramento	100* D	A.J. Foyt Jr.	Meskowski	Offy	4	252
11-20-60	Phoenix	100* D	A.J. Foyt Jr.	Meskowski	Offy	4	252
04-09-61	Trenton	100* P	Eddie Sachs	Kuzma	Offy	4	252
05-30-61	Indianapolis	500* P	A.J. Foyt Jr.	Trevis	Offy	4	252
06-04-61	Milwaukee	100* P	Rodger Ward	Watson	Offy	4	252
06-18-61	Langhorne	100* D	A.J. Foyt Jr.	Meskowski	Offy	4	252
08-20-61	Milwaukee	200* P	Lloyd Ruby	Watson	Offy	4	252
08-21-61	Springfield	99* D	Jim Hurtubise	Kuzma	Offy	4	252
09-04-61	DuQuoin	100* D	A.J. Foyt Jr.	Meskowski	Offy	4	252
09-09-61	Syracuse	100* D	Rodger Ward	Watson	Offy	4	252
09-16-61	Indianapolis	100* D	A.J. Foyt Jr.	Meskowski	Offy	4	252
09-24-61	Trenton	100* P	Eddie Sachs	Kuzma	Offy	4	252
10-29-61	Sacramento	100* D	Rodger Ward	Watson	Offy	4	252
11-19-61	Phoenix	89* D	Parnelli Jones	Kuzma	Offy	4	252
04-08-62	Trenton	100* P	A.J. Foyt Jr.	Meskowski	Offy	4	252
05-30-62	Indianapolis	500* P	Rodger Ward	Watson	Offy	4	252
06-10-62	Milwaukee	100* P	A.J. Foyt Jr.	Trevis	Offy	4	252
07-01-62	Langhorne	100* D	A.J. Foyt Jr.	Meskowski	Offy	4	252
07-22-62	Trenton	142* P	Rodger Ward	Watson	Offy	4	252
08-18-62	Springfield	100* D	Jim Hurtubise	Kuzma	Offy	4	252
08-19-62	Milwaukee	200* P	Rodger Ward	Watson	Offy	4	252
08-26-62	Langhorne	100* D	Don Branson	Watson	Offy	4	252
09-08-62	Syracuse	100* D	Rodger Ward	Watson	Offy	4	252
09-15-62	Indianapolis	100* D	Parnelli Jones	Kuzma	Offy	4	252
09-23-62	Trenton	200* P	Don Branson	Watson	Offy	4	252
10-28-62	Sacramento	100* D	A.J. Foyt Jr.	Meskowski	Offy	4	252
11-18-62	Phoenix	51* D	Bobby Marshman	Meskowski	Offy	4	252
04-21-63	Trenton	100* P	A.J. Foyt Jr.	Meskowski	Offy	4	252
05-30-63	Indianapolis	500* P	Parnelli Jones	Watson	Offy	4	252
06-09-63	Milwaukee	100* P	Rodger Ward	Watson	Offy	4	252
06-23-63	Langhorne	100* D	A.J. Foyt Jr.	Meskowski	Offy	4	252
07-28-63	Trenton	150* D	A.J. Foyt Jr.	Trevis	Offy	4	252
08-17-63	Springfield	100* D	Rodger Ward	Watson	Offy	4	252
09-02-63	DuQuoin	100* D	A.J. Foyt Jr.	Meskowski	Offy	4	252
09-14-63	Indianapolis	100* D	Rodger Ward	Watson	Offy	4	252
09-22-63	Trenton	200* P	A.J. Foyt Jr.	Trevis	Offy	4	252
10-27-63	Sacramento	100* D	Rodger Ward	Watson	Offy	4	252
11-17-63	Phoenix	100* D	Rodger Ward	Watson	Offy	4	252
03-22-64	Phoenix	100* P	A.J. Foyt Jr.	Trevis	Offy	4	252
04-19-64	Trenton	100* P	A.J. Foyt Jr.	Watson	Offy	4	252
05-30-64	Indianapolis	500* P	A.J. Foyt Jr.	Watson	Offy	4	252
06-07-64	Milwaukee	100* P	A.J. Foyt Jr.	Watson	Offy	4	252
06-21-64	Langhorne	100* D	A.J. Foyt Jr.	Meskowski	Offy	4	252
07-19-64	Trenton	150* P	A.J. Foyt Jr.	Watson	Offy	4	252

Date	Track	Miles	Winner	Chassis	Engine	Cyl.	CID
08-22-64	Springfield	100* D	A.J. Foyt Jr.	Meskowski	Offy	4	252
09-07-64	DuQuoin	100* D	A.J. Foyt Jr.	Meskowski	Offy	4	252
09-26-64	Indianapolis	100* D	A.J. Foyt Jr.	Meskowski	Offy	4	252
10-25-64	Sacramento	100* D	A.J. Foyt Jr.	Meskowski	Offy	4	252
11-22-64	Phoenix	200* P	Lloyd Ruby	Shrike	Offy	4	252
03-28-65	Phoenix	150* P	Don Branson	Watson	Offy	4	252
04-25-65	Trenton	87* P	Jim McElreath	Brabham	Offy	4	252
06-20-65	Langhorne	100* P	Jim McElreath	Brabham	Offy	4	252
08-08-65	Langhorne	125* P	Jim McElreath	Brabham	Offy	4	252
08-21-65	Springfield	100* D	A.J. Foyt Jr.	Meskowski	Offy	4	252
08-22-65	Milwaukee	200* P	Gordon Johncock	Gerhardt	Offy	4	252
09-06-65	DuQuoin	100* D	Don Branson	Watson	Offy	4	252
09-18-65	Indianapolis	100* D	A.J. Foyt Jr.	Meskowski	Offy	4	252
10-24-65	Sacramento	100* D	Don Branson	Watson	Offy	4	252
04-24-66	Trenton	102* P	Rodger Ward	Lola	Offy	4	168s
08-20-66	Springfield	100* D	Don Branson	Watson	Offy	4	252
09-05-66	DuQuoin	100* D	Bud Tingelstad	Meskowski	Offy	4	252
09-10-66	Indianapolis	100* D	Mario Andretti	Kuzma	Offy	4	252
10-23-66	Sacramento	100* D	Dick Atkins	Watson	Offy	4	252
04-09-67	Phoenix	150* P	Lloyd Ruby	Mongoose	Offy	4	168t
08-19-67	Springfield	100* D	A.J. Foyt Jr.	Meskowski	Offy	4	252
09-04-67	DuQuoin	100* D	A.J. Foyt Jr.	Meskowski	Offy	4	252
09-09-67	Indianapolis	100* D	Mario Andretti	Kuzma	Offy	4	252
10-01-67	Sacramento	100* D	A.J. Foyt Jr.	Meskowski	Offy	4	252
03-17-68	Hanford	201* P	Gordon Johncock	Gerhardt	Offy	4	168t
04-07-68	Phoenix	150* P	Bobby Unser	Eagle	Offy	4	168t
04-21-68	Trenton	150* P	Bobby Unser	Eagle	Offy	4	168t
05-30-68	Indianapolis	500* P	Bobby Unser	Eagle	Offy	4	168t
06-09-68	Milwaukee	150* P	Lloyd Ruby	Mongoose	Offy	4	168t
06-23-68	Langhorne	150* P	Gordon Johncock	Gerhardt	Offy	4	168t
07-13-68	Nazareth	100* D	Al Unser Sr.	Ward	Offy	4	252
08-17-68	Springfield	100* D	Roger McCluskey	Meskowski	Offy	4	252
08-18-68	Milwaukee	200* P	Lloyd Ruby	Mongoose	Offy	4	168t
09-02-68	DuQuoin	100* D	Mario Andretti	Kuzma	Offy	4	252
09-07-68	Indianapolis	100* D	A.J. Foyt Jr.	Meskowski	Offy	4	252
09-22-68	Trenton	200* P	Mario Andretti	Hawk	Offy	4	168t
09-29-68	Sacramento	100* D	A.J. Foyt Jr.	Meskowski	Offy	4	252
10-13-68	Michigan	250* P	Ronnie Bucknum	Eagle	Offy	4	168t
11-17-68	Phoenix	200* P	Gary Bettenhausen	Gerhardt	Offy	4	168t
06-08-69	Milwaukee	150* P	Art Pollard	Gerhardt	Offy	4	159t
06-22-69	Langhorne	150* P	Bobby Unser	Eagle	Offy	4	159t
07-12-69	Nazareth	100* D	Mario Andretti	Kuzma	Offy	4	252
08-18-69	Springfield	100* D	Mario Andretti	Kuzma	Offy	4	252
04-26-70	Trenton	201* P	Lloyd Ruby	Mongoose	Offy	4	159t
06-14-70	Langhorne	150* P	Bobby Unser	Eagle	Offy	4	159t
07-04-70	Michigan	200* P	Gary Bettenhausen	Gerhardt	Offy	4	159t
07-03-71	Pocono	500* P	Mark Donohue	McLaren	Offy	4	158t
07-18-71	Michigan	200* P	Mark Donohue	McLaren	Offy	4	158t
08-15-71	Milwaukee	200* P	Bobby Unser	Eagle	Offy	4	158t
10-03-71	Trenton	300* P	Bobby Unser	Eagle	Offy	4	158t
03-18-72	Phoenix	150* P	Bobby Unser	Eagle	Offy	4	158t
04-23-72	Trenton	201* P	Gary Bettenhausen	McLaren	Offy	4	158t
05-27-72	Indianapolis	500* P	Mark Donohue	McLaren	Offy	4	158t
06-04-72	Milwaukee	150* P	Bobby Unser	Eagle	Offy	4	158t
07-16-72	Michigan	200* P	Joe Leonard	Parnelli	Offy	4	158t
07-29-72	Pocono	500* P	Joe Leonard	Parnelli	Offy	4	158t
08-13-72	Milwaukee	200* P	Joe Leonard	Parnelli	Offy	4	158t
09-03-72	Ontario	500* P	Roger McCluskey	McLaren	Offy	4	158t
09-24-72	Trenton	300* P	Bobby Unser	Eagle	Offy	4	158t
11-04-72	Phoenix	150* P	Bobby Unser	Eagle	Offy	4	158t
04-07-73	Texas	200* P	Al Unser Sr.	Parnelli	Offy	4	158t
04-15-73	Trenton	150* P	Mario Andretti	Parnelli	Offy	4	158t
05-30-73	Indianapolis	333* P	Gordon Johncock	Eagle	Offy	4	159t
06-10-73	Milwaukee	150* P	Bobby Unser	Eagle	Offy	4	159t
07-15-73	Michigan	200* P	Roger McCluskey	McLaren	Offy	4	158t
08-12-73	Milwaukee	200* P	Wally Dallenbach	Eagle	Offy	4	159t
08-26-73	Ontario	100* P	Wally Dallenbach	Eagle	Offy	4	159t
08-26-73	Ontario	100* P	Johnny Rutherford	McLaren	Offy	4	158t
09-02-73	Ontario	500* P	Wally Dallenbach	Eagle	Offy	4	159t
09-16-73	Michigan	126* P	Billy Vukovich II	Eagle	Offy	4	158t
09-16-73	Michigan	126* P	Johnny Rutherford	McLaren	Offy	4	158t
09-23-73	Trenton	201* P	Gordon Johncock	Eagle	Offy	4	159t
10-06-73	Texas	200* P	Gary Bettenhausen	McLaren	Offy	4	158t
11-03-73	Phoenix	150* P	Gordon Johncock	Eagle	Offy	4	159t
03-03-74	Ontario	100* P	Johnny Rutherford	McLaren	Offy	4	158t
03-10-74	Ontario	500* P	Bobby Unser	Eagle	Offy	4	159t
03-17-74	Phoenix	150* P	Mike Mosley	Eagle	Offy	4	158t
04-07-74	Trenton	201* P	Bobby Unser	Eagle	Offy	4	159t
05-26-74	Indianapolis	500* P	Johnny Rutherford	McLaren	Offy	4	158t

Date	Track	Miles	Winner	Chassis	Engine	Cyl.	CID
06-09-74	Milwaukee	150* P	Johnny Rutherford	McLaren	Offy	4	158t
06-30-74	Pocono	500* P	Johnny Rutherford	McLaren	Offy	4	158t
07-21-74	Michigan	200* P	Bobby Unser	Eagle	Offy	4	159t
08-11-74	Milwaukee	200* P	Gordon Johncock	Eagle	Offy	4	159t
09-15-74	Michigan	250* P	Al Unser Sr.	Eagle	Offy	4	158t
09-22-74	Trenton	150* P	Bobby Unser	Eagle	Offy	4	159t
11-02-74	Phoenix	150* P	Gordon Johncock	Eagle	Offy	4	159t
03-02-75	Ontario	100* P	Wally Dallenbach	Eagle	Offy	4	159t
03-16-75	Phoenix	150* P	Johnny Rutherford	McLaren	Offy	4	158t
05-25-75	Indianapolis	435* P	Bobby Unser	Eagle	Offy	4	159t
08-17-75	Milwaukee	200* P	Mike Mosley	Eagle	Offy	4	158t
09-13-75	Michigan	150* P	Tom Sneva	McLaren	Offy	4	158t
09-21-75	Trenton	150* P	Gordon Johncock	Wildcat	DGS	4	158t
03-14-76	Phoenix	150* P	Bobby Unser	Eagle	Offy	4	158t
05-02-76	Trenton	201* P	Johnny Rutherford	McLaren	Offy	4	158t
05-30-76	Indianapolis	255* P	Johnny Rutherford	McLaren	Offy	4	158t
06-13-76	Milwaukee	150* P	Mike Mosley	Eagle	Offy	4	158t
07-18-76	Michigan	200* P	Gordon Johncock	Wildcat	DGS	4	158t
08-15-76	Trenton	176* P	Gordon Johncock	Wildcat	DGS	4	158t
09-05-76	Ontario	500* P	Bobby Unser	Eagle	Offy	4	158t
10-31-76	Texas	200* P	Johnny Rutherford	McLaren	Offy	4	158t
04-30-77	Trenton	201* P	Wally Dallenbach	Wildcat	DGS	4	158t
09-17-77	Michigan	150* P	Gordon Johncock	Wildcat	DGS	4	158t
10-29-77	Phoenix	150* P	Gordon Johncock	Wildcat	DGS	4	158t
03-18-78	Phoenix	150* P	Gordon Johncock	Wildcat	DGS	4	158t
04-23-78	Trenton	201* P	Gordon Johncock	Wildcat	DGS	4	158t

NOTE: The DGS (Drake-Goossen-Sparks) engine had a narrower valve angle of 44 degrees as opposed to the original design's 72 degrees. The redesign of the valve angle was begun by Leo Goossen in 1973 and completed by Hans Hermann in time for the 1975 season. This change was first conceived by Art Sparks, hence the name of the engine.

For the 1976 season, another redesign by Hermann resulted in the valve angle being further reduced to 38 degrees. This engine was named an Offy.

Miller-Offy Silver Crown Car Winners

Date	Track	Miles	Winner	Chassis	Engine	Cyl.	CID
09-06-71	DuQuoin	100* D	George Snider	Watson	Offy	4	252
09-07-74	Indianapolis	100* D	Jackie Howerton	King	Offy	4	158t

Miller-Offy National Championship Winners

1921	Tommy Milton
1922	Jimmy Murphy
1923	Eddie Hearne
1924	Jimmy Murphy
1926	Harry Hartz
1927	Peter De Paolo
1928	Louis Meyer
1929	Louis Meyer
1930	Billy Arnold
1931	Louis Schneider
1932	Bob Carey
1933	Louis Meyer
1934	Bill Cummings
1935	Kelly Petillo
1936	Mauri Rose
1937	Wilbur Shaw
1938	Floyd Roberts
1940	Rex Mays
1941	Rex Mays
1946	Ted Horn
1947	Ted Horn
1948	Ted Horn
1949	Johnnie Parsons
1950	Henry Banks
1951	Tony Bettenhausen
1952	Chuck Stevenson
1953	Sam Hanks
1954	Jimmy Bryan
1955	Bob Sweikert
1956	Jimmy Bryan
1957	Jimmy Bryan
1958	Tony Bettenhausen
1959	Rodger Ward
1960	A.J. Foyt Jr.
1961	A.J. Foyt Jr.
1962	Rodger Ward
1963	A.J. Foyt Jr.
1964	A.J. Foyt Jr.
1968	Bobby Unser
1972	Joe Leonard
1973	Roger McCluskey
1974	Bobby Unser
1976	Gordon Johncock

Miller-Offy Pacific Coast Championship Winners

1930	Francis Quinn
1931	Ernie Triplett
1932	Ernie Triplett
1933	Al Gordon
1935	Rex Mays

Miller-Offy Championship Engine Wins

Engine	Cyl.	CID	Championship Wins	Non-Championship Wins
Pre-World War II				
Miller	4	289	0	3
Miller	8	181	16	5
Miller	8	121	12	1
Miller	8	121s	9	13
Miller	8	151	6	2
Miller	8	182	1	0
Miller	8	91s	1	3
Miller	8	90s	35	17
Miller	8	101s	0	1
Miller	8	90	0	1
Miller Marine	4	150s	1	6
Miller Marine	4	150	2	0
Miller	8	230	3	0
Miller	8	249	2	0
Miller	8	258	1	0
Miller	8	268	3	0
Miller	4	220	5	0
Miller	4	228	0	1
Miller	4	255	5	0
Offy	4	262	3	0
Offy	4	255	3	0
Offy	4	270	4	0
Sparks	4	269	1	0
Sparks	4	239	1	0
Sparks	4	203	0	2
Winfield	8	180s	4	0
Post-World War II				
Offy	4	270	86	
Offy	4	255	3	
Offy	4	241	9	
Offy	4	263	9	
Offy	4	233	6	
Offy	4	107s	4	
Sparks	6	183s	1	
Sparks	4	203	1	
Winfield	8	180s	3	
Offy	4	250	1	
Offy	4	252	118 (includes one Silver Crown win)	
Offy	4	255	5	
Offy	4	166s	1	
Offy	4	168s	1	
Offy	4	168t	11	
Offy	4	159t	20	
Offy	4	158t	37 (includes one Silver Crown win)	
SGD	4	158t	8	

Miller-Offy Pacific Coast Championship Engine Wins

Engine	Cyl.	CID	Wins
Pre-World War II			
Miller Marine	4	150	2
Miller Marine	4	182	21
Miller Marine	4	207	4
Miller-Schofield	4	200	2
Miller-Schofield	4	214	15
Cragar	4	200	21
Miller	4	200	14
Miller	4	220	80
Miller	8	249	2
Miller	4	255	6
Sparks	4	203	26

Appendix V: Miller and Offenhauser at Indianapolis

Year	Best Finish	Percentage of Top Ten	Percentage of Starting Field	Year	Best Finish	Percentage of Top Ten	Percentage of Starting Field
1921	7	10	4	1953	1	100	97
1922	1	10	15	1954	1	100	100
1923	1	60	46	1955	1	100	100
1924	2	80	64	1956	1	100	97
1925	2	60	73	1957	1	90	94
1926	1	90	71	1958	1	90	94
1927	2	80	85	1959	1	100	100
1928	1	90	83	1960	1	100	100
1929	1	70	82	1961	1	90	97
1930	1	70	47	1962	1	100	97
1931	1	40	40	1963	1	70	79
1932	1	30	45	1964	1	100	73
1933	1	40	48	1965	5	30	42
1934	1	60	55	1966	5	30	27
1935	1	100	82	1967	7	20	27
1936	1	90	94	1968	1	80	42
1937	1	90	79	1969	3	40	61
1938	1	100	70	1970	3	40	45
1939	3	50	58	1971	2	60	52
1940	3	40	58	1972	1	60	67
1941	1	60	61	1973	1	90	82
1946	2	50	48	1974	1	80	85
1947	1	40	53	1975	1	90	88
1948	1	70	70	1976	1	80	91
1949	1	100	85	1977	4	70	73
1950	1	100	97	1978	3	40	58
1951	1	90	94	1979	7	20	37
1952	1	100	88	1980	3	10	15

Appendix VI: Miller Car and Engine Speed Records

Researched and compiled by Joseph Freeman

Distance	Type	Date	Place	Driver	Car	Engine	CID	MPH	Record
1 M	S	4-4-24	Munroc Dry Lake	Tom Milton	Miller	Miller 8	181	151.26	Intl Class D
1 M	S	4-4-24	Munroc Dry Lake	Tom Milton	Miller	Miller 8	121	141.17	Intl Class E*
5 M	CC	3-21-26	Los Angeles	Bennett Hill	Miller	Miller 8	121	137.931	US Class E*
10 M	CC	3-21-26	Los Angeles	Leon Duray	Miller	Miller 8	121	136.054	US Class E*
25 M	CC	5-1-26	Atlantic City	Bob McDonough	Miller	Miller 8	121	137.426	US Class E*
50 M	CC	5-1-26	Atlantic City	Bob McDonough	Miller	Miller 8	121	135.890	US Class E*
100 M	CC	3-21-26	Los Angeles	Dave Lewis	Miller FD	Miller 8	121	133.709	US Class E*
200 M	CC	5-1-26	Atlantic City	Bob McDonough	Miller	Miller 8	121	132.375	US Class E*
250 M	CC	5-1-26	Atlantic City	Bob McDonough	Miller	Miller 8	121	134.068	US Class E*
300 M	CC	5-1-26	Atlantic City	Harry Hartz	Miller	Miller 8	121	134.091	US Class E*
400 M	CC	5-30-25	Indianapolis	Dave Lewis	Miller FD	Miller 8	121	101.16	US Class E*
5 K	CC	9-1-26	Montlhéry	E.A.D. Eldridge	Miller	Miller 8	121 s	125.59	Intl Class E
5 M	CC	9-1-26	Montlhéry	E.A.D. Eldridge	Miller	Miller 8	121 s	122.38	Intl Class E
1 M	S	9-5-26	Arpajon	E.A.D. Eldridge	Miller	Miller 8	121 s	136.26	Intl Class E
10 M	CC	9-7-26	Montlhéry	E.A.D. Eldridge	Miller	Miller 8	121 s	131.75	Intl Class E
5 M	CC	9-21-26	Montlhéry	E.A.D. Eldridge	Miller	Miller 8	90 s	133.24	Intl Class F
10 K	CC	9-21-26	Montlhéry	E.A.D. Eldridge	Miller	Miller 8	90 s	138.92	Intl Class F
10 M	CC	9-21-26	Montlhéry	E.A.D. Eldridge	Miller	Miller 8	90 s	132.47	Intl Class F
50 K	CC	12-31-26	Montlhéry	E.A.D. Eldridge	Miller	Miller 8	121 s	123.9	Intl Class E
50 M	CC	12-31-26	Montlhéry	E.A.D. Eldridge	Miller	Miller 8	121 s	124.8	Intl Class E
100 k	CC	12-31-26	Montlhéry	E.A.D. Eldridge	Miller	Miller 8	121 s	126.8	Intl Class E
100 M	CC	12-31-26	Montlhéry	E.A.D. Eldridge	Miller	Miller 8	121 s	127.1	Intl Class E
1 Hr.	CC	12-31-26	Montlhéry	E.A.D. Eldridge	Miller	Miller 8	121 s	126.51	Intl Class E
100 M	CC	4-27	Montlhéry	Douglas Hawkes	Miller	Miller 8	90 s	113.48	Intl Class F
1 Hr.	CC	4-27	Montlhéry	Douglas Hawkes	Miller	Miller 8	90 s	113.34	Intl Class F
1 M	S	4-11-27	Muroc Dry Lake	Frank Lockhart	Miller	Miller 8	90 s	164.84	Intl Class F
1.5 M	CC	5-7-27	Atlantic City	Frank Lockhart	Miller	Miller 8	90 s	147.729	Intl Class F*
5 M	CC	5-7-27	Atlantic City	Frank Lockhart	Miller	Miller 8	90 s	133.560	US Class F*
10 M	CC	5-7-27	Atlantic City	Frank Lockhart	Miller	Miller 8	90 s	135.659	US Class F*
25 M	CC	11-11-26	Charlotte	Frank Lockhart	Miller	Miller 8	90 s	132.405	US Class F*
50 M	CC	5-7-27	Atlantic City	Dave Lewis	Miller FD	Miller 8	90 s	131.075	US Class F*
100 M	CC	9-16-28	Atlantic City	Ray Keech	Miller	Miller 8	90 s	131.805	US Class F*
200 M	CC	5-7-27	Atlantic City	Dave Lewis	Miller FD	Miller 8	90 s	130.058	US Class F*
250 M	CC	3-6-27	Los Angeles	Leon Duray	Miller FD	Miller 8	90 s	124.712	US Class F*
400 M	CC	5-30-28	Indianapolis	Tony Gulotta	Miller	Miller 8	90 s	100.988	US Class F*
500 M	CC	5-30-28	Indianapolis	Louis Meyer	Miller	Miller 8	90 s	99.482	US Class F*
0.5 M	CC	10-14-27	Salem, NH	Frank Lockhart	Miller	Miller 8	90 s	137.091	Intl Class F**
1 M	CC	10-14-27	Salem, NH	Frank Lockhart	Miller	Miller 8	90 s	134.279	Intl Class F**
		(Frank Lockhart set various Class F records on this date at distances between 1 mile and 10 miles)							
10 M	CC	10-14-27	Salem, NH	Frank Lockhart	Miller	Miller 8	90 s	131.492	Intl Class F**
1 Hr.	CC	6-6-28	Brooklands	Harold Purdy	Lea-Francis	Miller 8	90 s	110.63	Brit Class E
1 M	S	4-25-28	Daytona Beach	Frank Lockhart	Stutz	Miller V-16	180 s	198.29	US Class D***
2.5 M	CC	6-6-28	Packard Track	Leon Duray	Miller FD	Miller 8	90 s	148.17	Intl Class F
5 M	CC-SS	8-10-29	Montlhéry	Leon Duray	Miller FD	Miller 8	90 s	137.22	Intl Class F
10 M	CC-SS	8-10-29	Montlhéry	Leon Duray	Miller FD	Miller 8	90 s	135.33	Intl Class F
1 K	S	8-25-29	Arpajon	Leon Duray	Miller FD	Miller 8	90 s	143.30	Intl Class F
1 M	S	8-25-29	Arpajon	Leon Duray	Miller FD	Miller 8	90 s	131.78	Intl Class F
5 K	CC-SS	9-1-29	Montlhéry	Leon Duray	Miller FD	Miller 8	90 s	139.55	Intl Class F
5 M	CC-SS	9-1-29	Montlhéry	Leon Duray	Miller FD	Miller 8	90 s	139.22	Intl Class F
1 M	S	4-30	Muroc Dry Lake	Shorty Cantlon	Miller	Schofield 4	183	141.75	Intl Class D
1 M	S	4-30	Muroc Dry Lake	Shorty Cantlon	Miller	Schofield 4	183 s	144.89	Intl Class D
100 M	CC	8-30	Montlhéry	Gwenda Stewart	Miller FD	Miller 8	90 s	118.13	Intl Class F

Distance	Type	Date	Place	Driver	Car	Engine	CID	MPH	Record
1 Hr	CC	8-30	Montlhéry	Gwenda Stewart	Miller FD	Miller 8	90 s	118.29	Intl Class F
200 K	CC	8-30	Montlhéry	Gwenda Stewart	Miller FD	Miller 8	90 s	118.32	Intl Class F
5 K	CC	9-10-30	Montlhéry	Gwenda Stewart	Miller FD	Miller 8	121 s	129.01	Intl Class E
5 M	CC	9-10-30	Montlhéry	Gwenda Stewart	Miller FD	Miller 8	121 s	128.14	Intl Class E
100 K	CC	12-30	Montlhéry	Gwenda Stewart	Miller FD	Miller 8	121 s	128.06	Intl Class E
1 M	S	8-30-31	Pismo Beach	Stubby Stubblefield	Miller	Cragar 4	207	130	Intl Class C?
1 K	S	8-30-31	Pismo Beach	Ernie Triplett	Miller	Schofield 4	213	130.7	Intl Class C?
10 M	CC	4-3-31	Montlhéry	Gwenda Stewart	Miller FD	Miller 8	121 s	134.26	Intl Class E
5 K	CC	4-7-31	Montlhéry	Gwenda Stewart	Miller FD	Miller 8	121 s	139.80	Intl Class E
5 M	CC	4-7-31	Montlhéry	Gwenda Stewart	Miller FD	Miller 8	121 s	139.41	Intl Class E
50 K	CC-SS	7-8-31	Montlhéry	Gwenda Stewart	Miller FD	Miller 8	121 s	126.81	Intl Class E
50 M	CC-SS	7-8-31	Montlhéry	Gwenda Stewart	Miller FD	Miller 8	121 s	127.97	Intl Class E
100 K	CC-SS	7-8-31	Montlhéry	Gwenda Stewart	Miller FD	Miller 8	121 s	128.16	Intl Class E
1 M	CC	3-22-32	Muroc Dry Lake	Wilbur Shaw	Miller	Miller 4	220	137.252	Intl Class C
1 K	S	5-16-32	Muroc Dry Lake	Stubby Stubblefield	Sparks	Miller 4	220	148.218	Intl Class C
1 M	S	5-16-32	Muroc Dry Lake	Stubby Stubblefield	Sparks	Miller 4	220	148.355	Intl Class C
5 K	S	5-16-32	Muroc Dry Lake	Stubby Stubblefield	Sparks	Miller 4	220	133.985	Intl Class C
5 M	S	5-16-32	Muroc Dry Lake	Stubby Stubblefield	Sparks	Miller 4	220	133.28	Intl Class C
1 K	S	3-9-12-33	Muroc Dry Lake	Harry Hartz	Adams	Miller 4	255	149.80	Intl Class C
1 M	S	3-9-12-33	Muroc Dry Lake	Harry Hartz	Adams	Miller 4	255	152.10	Intl Class C

(Harry Hartz and Fred Frame set various Class C records on these dates between the distances of 1 mile and 50 miles.)

Distance	Type	Date	Place	Driver	Car	Engine	CID	MPH	Record
50 M	S	3-9-12-33	Muroc Dry Lake	Fred Frame	Adams	Miller 4	255	144.63	Intl Class C
1 M	CC	4-5-33	Montlhéry	Gwenda Stewart	Miller FD	Miller 8	122 s	137.85	Intl Class E
1 M	CC	5-2-33	Montlhéry	Gwenda Stewart	Miller FD	Miller 8	122 s	139.13	Intl Class E
1 M	CC	5-19-33	Montlhéry	Gwenda Stewart	Miller FD	Miller 8	122 s	143.29	Intl Class E
10 M	CC	9-1-33	Montlhéry	Gwenda Stewart	Miller FD	Miller 8	122 s	138.34	Intl Class E
5 K	CC	4-14-34	Montlhéry	Gwenda Stewart	Miller FD	Miller 8	122 s	140.351	Intl Class E
5 M	CC	4-14-34	Montlhéry	Gwenda Stewart	Miller FD	Miller 8	122 s	140.17	Intl Class E
10 K	CC	4-14-34	Montlhéry	Gwenda Stewart	Miller FD	Miller 8	122 s	140.07	Intl Class E
1 K	CC	7-25-34	Montlhéry	Gwenda Stewart	Miller FD	Miller 8	122 s	143.29	Intl Class E
1 M	CC	7-25-34	Montlhéry	Gwenda Stewart	Miller FD	Miller 8	122 s	147.79	Intl Class E
2.77 M	CC	8-6-35	Brooklands	Gwenda Stewart	Miller FD	Miller 8	122 s	135.95	Brit Class E
1 M	S	4-18-37	Muroc Dry Lake	Ron Householder	Wetteroth	Offy 4	98	123.29	US Class E
1 K	S	7-30-40	Bonneville	George Barringer	Miller 4 WD	Miller 6	180 s	157.563	US Class D
5 K	S	7-30-40	Bonneville	George Barringer	Miller 4WD	Miller 6	180 s	158.446	Intl Class D
5 M	S	7-30-40	Bonneville	George Barringer	Miller 4WD	Miller 6	180 s	158.207	Intl Class D
10 K	CC	7-30-40	Bonneville	George Barringer	Miller 4WD	Miller 6	180 s	153.237	Intl Class D

(Barringer set various closed course Class D records on this date between the distances of 10 kilometers and 500 miles.)

Distance	Type	Date	Place	Driver	Car	Engine	CID	MPH	Record
500 M	CC	7-30-40	Bonneville	George Barringer	Miller 4WD	Miller 6	180 s	142.799	Intl Class D
3 Hrs	CC	7-30-40	Bonneville	George Barringer	Miller 4WD	Miller 6	180 s	142.39	Intl Class D
1 M	S	8-47	Bonneville	Danny Oakes	Lesovsky	Offy 4	105	139.436	
1 K	S	9-14-49	Bonneville	Rex Mays	Lesovsky	Offy 4	105	147.105	US Class E
1 M	S	9-14-49	Bonneville	Rex Mays	Lesovsky	Offy 4	105	147.307	US Class E
1 M	S	10-2-88	Bonneville	Gordon E. White	Kurtis	Offy 4	121.5	156.902	US Midget
1 M	S	8-23-89	Bonneville	Gordon E. White	Kurtis	Offy 4	121.5	153.198	Intl Class A-II-7
1 M	S	8-88	Bonneville	Jim Lattin		Offy 4	270	166.940	US Vintage Record

NOTES:

All runs Flying Start except where indicated.
Type: S = Straightaway; CC = Closed Course; SS = Standing Start
CID: s = supercharged
  * These records represent the fastest performances for various distances set on American speedways during races sanctioned and timed by the AAA. They were not recognised by international authorities at that time.
 ** "Non-Competitive" records set by Lockhart during a special AAA-administered run at the Rockingham board track speedway.
*** This US record was the result of a one-way timed run and did not break the international mark.

Bibliography

Banning, Gene. *Speedway—Half a Century of Racing With Art Sparks*. Incline Village, Nevada: Spartus, 1983.

Bloemker, Al. *500 Miles to Go*. New York: Coward-McCann, 1961.

Borgeson, Griffith. *The Classic Twin Cam Engine*. London, England: Dalton Watson, 1981.

Borgeson, Griffith. *Errett Lobban Cord—His Empire, His Motor Cars. Auburn, Cord, Duesenberg*. Princeton, New Jersey: Automobile Quarterly, 1984.

Borgeson, Griffith. "Fresh Footnotes to the History of Miller Front-wheel Drive." Princeton, New Jersey: *Automobile Quarterly* 21 (1983): 4.

Borgeson, Griffith. *The Golden Age of the American Racing Car*. New York: Norton, Bonanza, 1966.

Borgeson, Griffith. "The Pre-conquest Millers." Princeton, New Jersey: *Automobile Quarterly* 19 (1981): 1.

Clymer, Floyd. *Indianapolis Racing History*. Los Angeles: Clymer, 1945.

Clymer, Floyd. *Indianapolis Yearbooks, 1949–1968*. Los Angeles: Clymer.

Dees, Mark. *The Miller Dynasty*. Scarsdale, New York: Barnes, 1981.

Dees, Mark. "Of Submarines and Time Machines: The Golden Sub Reborn." Princeton, New Jersey: *Automobile Quarterly* 23 (1985): 1.

De Paolo, Peter. *Wall Smacker*. Cleveland, Ohio: Thompson, 1935.

Fox, Jack C. *The Indianapolis 500*. Speedway, Indiana: Hungness, 1975.

Fox, Jack C. *The Mighty Midgets*. Speedway, Indiana: Hungness, 1977.

Hungness, Carl. *Indianapolis Yearbook*. Los Angeles, California: Hungness, 1973-on.

Huntington, Roger. *Design and Development of the Indy Car*. Los Angeles, California: HP Books, 1981.

Levine, Leo. *Ford: The Dust and the Glory*. New York: Macmillan, 1968.

O'Keefe, James, and Joseph Freeman. *Encyclopedia of Auto Racing Winners*. In preparation.

Shaw, Wilbur. *Gentlemen, Start Your Engines*. New York: Coward-McCann, 1955.

Wagner, Fred J. *Saga of the Roaring Road*. Los Angeles, California: Clymer, 1949.

Wallen, Dick. *Board Track—Guts, Gold and Glory*. Escondido, California: Wallen, 1990.

Walton, Kenneth E. *Offy—America's Greatest Racing Engine*. In preparation.

Index of Names